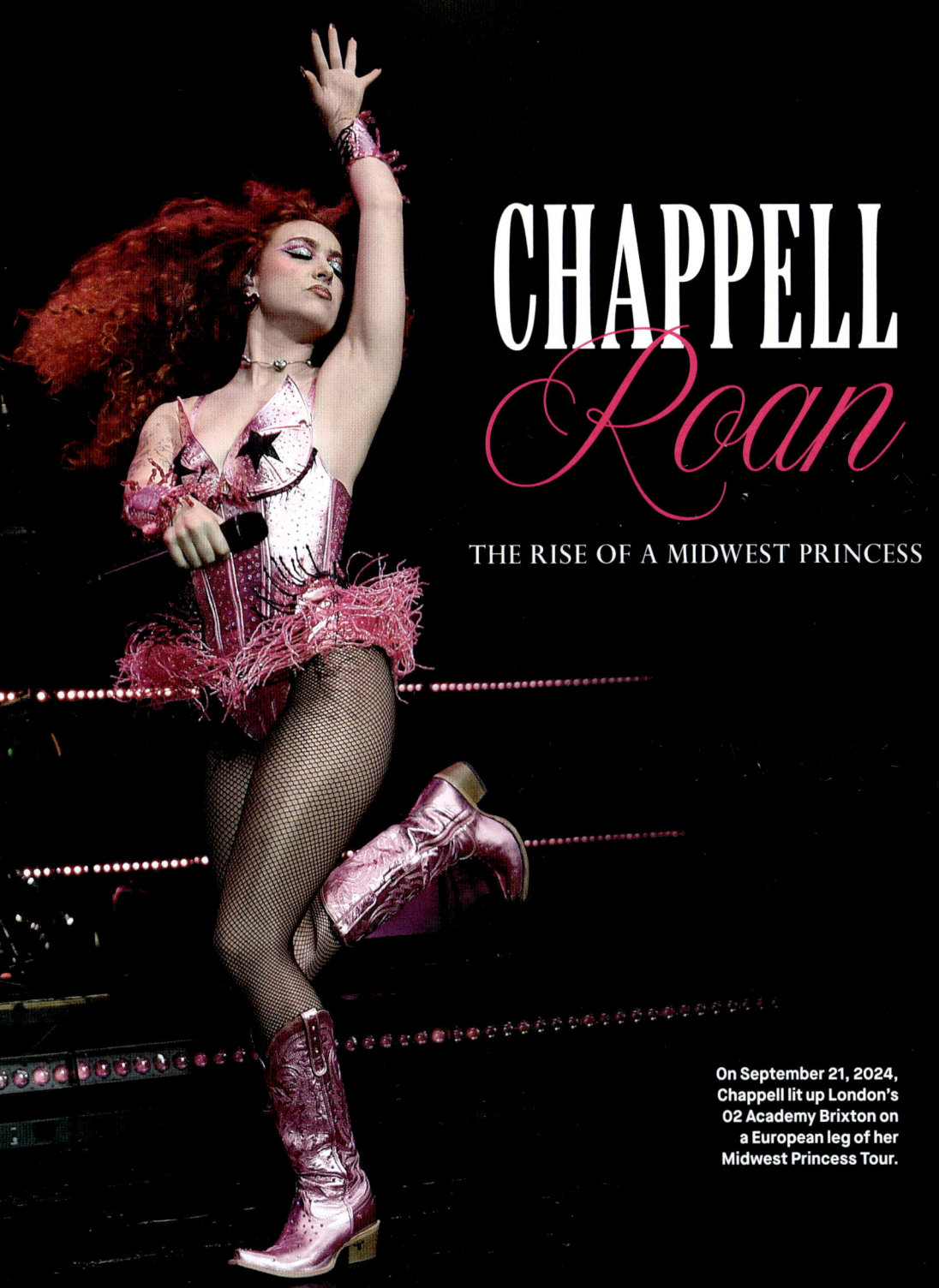

CHAPPELL
Roan

THE RISE OF A MIDWEST PRINCESS

On September 21, 2024, Chappell lit up London's 02 Academy Brixton on a European leg of her Midwest Princess Tour.

Chappell, on the cusp of stardom, in her dressing room at Chicago's House of Blues on October 5, 2023.

CHAPPELL *Roan*

THE RISE OF A MIDWEST PRINCESS

JENNIFER KEISHIN ARMSTRONG, DIBS BAER, TRISH BENDIX, KATHERINE CONLON,
PATRICK CROWLEY, IZZY GRINSPAN, J'NA JEFFERSON, LAURA KALEHOFF,
ILANA KAPLAN, JENNIFER RAINEY MARQUEZ, SAMANTHA OLSON,
ROCKY RAKOVIC, CHELSEY SANCHEZ, AND PENELOPE WHITBOURNE

HEARST
HOME

Contents

Chappell was her own makeup artist back in the day, like on October 5, 2023, at Chicago's House of Blues. Her longtime favorite products include Benefit Roller Lash Curling & Lifting Mascara. "I use it on tour every night," she told *Elle* magazine.

Chappell's set at House of Blues in Chicago on October 5, 2023, included 15 of her own songs plus a cover of Lady Gaga's "Bad Romance."

Her Story

RISE OF A MIDWEST PRINCESS

She's a FEMININOMENON!

by Jennifer Keishin Armstrong
New York Times best-selling author and pop culture historian

CHAPPELL Roan is, quite simply, a generational musical talent. At Coachella in April 2024, she confidently introduced herself as "your favorite artist's favorite artist"—the least humble brag one could imagine. Chappell's line referenced a moment from *RuPaul's Drag Race*, where guest judge Sasha Colby declared, "I am your favorite drag queen's favorite drag queen." Chappell wasn't wrong. Since then, she's snagged the attention of no less than the Recording Academy (which awarded her Best New Artist Award at the 2025 Grammys), Sir Elton John and other music greats, and millions of fans around the world.

Chappell seemed to have come out of nowhere in the summer of 2024. The truth is anything but. Just a few years earlier, she was struggling as an artist in Los Angeles, secretly hoping her dad would pick her up and take her back home to Missouri. Then, one night, friends brought her to The Abbey, a storied Los Angeles gay bar featuring go-go dancers on stages. "Overwhelmed with complete love and acceptance," she told *Headliner* that the "spiritual experience" inspired her to write the breakthrough song, "Pink Pony Club." In it, she mimics a mother figure, having discovered her child's unsavory employment: "God, what have you done? You're a Pink Pony girl, and you dance at the club." Oh, the humanity! Anyone who grew up in the Midwest (myself included) understands the sentiment of this Chappell lyric.

Her other major songs continue the themes of queer exploration, rebellion, and reinvention, from "Naked in Manhattan," a tale of seducing a secret high school crush of the same sex, to "Red Wine Supernova," an ode to a hot girl who was "a Playboy, Brigitte Bardot..." who "put her canine teeth in the side of my neck," to "Good Luck, Babe!" a lament for a girl she lost to a boy.

In the short span of one festival season, Chappell went suddenly, improbably, ultra-mainstream. By August 2024, she had a startling seven songs on the Billboard Hot 100. The long history of closeted pop stars suggests that Chappell's authenticity shouldn't have worked to this level. The music industry, after all, has never seemed particularly invested in promoting queer and gay artists, making her success particularly staggering. (Many of us can remember a time when George Michael felt pressured to act aggressively straight, even while singing "Father Figure" somehow.) One can imagine the record company executives in suits explaining to Chappell why kiss-offs and sexually explicit come-ons expressly directed at girls aren't marketable. What is this about being "knee deep in the passenger seat, and you're eating me out"? Must she complain in "My Kink Is Karma" that her former lover "stole my cute aesthetic," clearly marking that lover as female? In "Good Luck, Babe!" is it necessary to describe a lost love so specifically as kissing "a hundred boys in bars," obviously escaping her for heterosexuality?

Chappell's alt-indie EP, *School Nights,* blends electronic beats with acoustic elements, creating a lush backdrop for her musings on toxic love ("Good Hurt") and the sweetness of reciprocity ("Sugar High"). The five-song project was released on September 22, 2017, under her former label, Atlantic Records, and clocks in at just under 18 minutes long. Though short, it's a glimpse into her budding artistry. The album art, designed by British artist Abbey Lila, captures the ethereal, smoky essence of her sound. (Chappell herself thanked the artist on Facebook in 2017 "for making my dreams come true.") Upon its release, *PopCrush* compared Chappell to Lana Del Rey, but noted that she "exudes an air of teenage mystique and emotional rawness all her own."

The fact is, I'm a straight woman, but that doesn't stop me from relating to Chappell's music. The vulnerable thoughts she expresses about love, independence, and longing are universal. Here's one of my favorite verses, from "Hot to Go!" "I could be the one, or your new addiction / It's all in my head but I want non-fiction." I may have screamed aloud the first time I heard these lyrics. Have you ever felt as if someone had taken pages from your diary, made them better, and then written them into a banger of a song?

In some ways, we've been working toward Chappell for a while. Her outrageous style recalls Cher and Lady Gaga; her vocal acrobatics and command of dynamics are reminiscent of Kate Bush and Cyndi Lauper; her precise songwriting echoes Taylor Swift and Olivia Rodrigo (the latter with whom she shares a collaborating producer, Dan Nigro); her explicit lyrics recall Prince. And women like Melissa Etheridge, Tegan and Sara, and Janelle Monáe have sung about their love for other women. But no one has put it all together quite like Chappell. In an America where rights are being taken systematically, deliberately from women and queer people, Chappell's rise feels bigger, more meaningful, than just a fun "Hot to Go!" dance.

Celebrating "girl power" has been all but mandatory for female pop stars since the Spice Girls burst onto the scene in the '90s. Before that, other female pop stars turned in some great (at times truly brave) empowerment anthems such as Lesley Gore's "You Don't Own Me" (1963), Aretha Franklin's "Respect" (1967), Helen Reddy's "I Am Woman" (1971), Gloria Gaynor's "I Will Survive" (1978), and Cyndi Lauper's "Girls Just Want to Have Fun" (1983). Chappell represents a radical version of girl power—in part because she's building on their work. However, at every turn, she takes the quest for liberation further and makes it her own, setting apart her uniquely 2020s pop star feminism.

SHE'S A STEP BEYOND QUEER PRIDE

Chappell brings a Gen Z nonchalance to her outness. She's not writing gay anthems; she's writing about her own experience. She's having such a good time, even with all the dating drama, that she makes being a queer woman seem fun, even superior to straightness. It's reminiscent of how *Sex and the City* turned single womanhood from a curse to the most desired lifestyle in the land. Chappell's rise coincided with the coming out of established pop genius Billie Eilish, whose single "Lunch" is also about being into girls. Same-sex sex is no longer a deal-breaker in the Top 40, a huge and welcome change for the creativity that has been unleashed.

SHE'S AN ASTUTE CULTURAL CRITIC

Chappell recognizes how straightness can weigh on women in a patriarchal society. Pick any Chappell song, and there's a good chance you'll get some sick anti-straight-guy burns. Take this line from "Femininomenon," for example:

> *Stuck in the suburbs, you're folding his laundry*
> *Got what you wanted, so stop feeling sorry*

Or this one from "Super Graphic Ultra Modern Girl":

> *Uh-huh, I'm through*
> *With all these hyper mega bummer boys like you*

Or this biting line from "Good Luck, Babe!":

> *When you wake up next to him in the middle of the night*
> *With your head in your hands, you're nothing more than his wife*

In Chappell's world, men are useless at best; in fact, they are often a hindrance. Her biggest songs are roaring odes to female power—because she's deliriously in love with women. "Red Wine Supernova" swoons over a girl with long hair and no bra ("that's my type") and offers a "wand and a rabbit" as an enticement to come over. According to "Femininomenon," only women can "hit it like rom-pom-pom-pom" and "get it hot like Papa John." The choruses of these songs soar and thump with a power you feel in your body, and hearing appreciation for the female form through a female gaze just hits different. There's no creepy objectification, only the thrill of realizing that women are glorious.

Karmella Uchawi was one of two drag queens Chappell chose to open for her at the Midland Theatre in Kansas City, Missouri, on April 8, 2024, on the Midwest Princess Tour. "It's just a great way to engage the local queer community," she explained to *People* in 2023. "I encourage people to tip the queens, that's redistributing funds within the community there, and also it just gives a platform for the drag queens. Some of these queens have never performed in front of a crowd that big before, and it's just fun."

SHE'S CASUALLY SEX POSITIVE

Chappell's not aggressively graphic, but she's not holding back, either. She follows that "knee-deep in the passenger seat" line in "Casual" with this heartbreaker: "Two weeks and your mom invites me to her house in Long Beach / Is it casual now?" The juxtaposition of physical intimacy and emotional intimacy, while the relationship is being declared "casual," is the killer here. Genders don't matter; the anguish of the situation is palpable and relatable. Meanwhile, the joy of impending sex in "Red Wine Supernova" is contagious.

SHE'S INSPIRED BY DRAG QUEENS

Though she's a cis woman, she takes inspiration from folks who appreciate the divine feminine. Her drag-like look is pure camp—a longstanding queer tradition—while making it clear that she's not interested in appealing to straight men. Chappell booked drag queens as her tour openers and is inspired by them in her own hair, dress, and makeup. "I've never fully understood why women shouldn't be allowed to do drag because—yes, I do drag!" she told German publication *Annabelle*. "It feels like they don't like women doing certain things. Another man trying to tell a woman what to do. Just try telling me what to do! I'm a drag queen—whether you like it if women do it or not." Significantly, she broke through to the mainstream with this aesthetic at a time when drag queens are being politically vilified and targeted.

SHE LIKES CHEERLEADERS, TOO

On songs like "Hot to Go!" Chappell co-opts this classically feminine, American archetype to exalt female energy and get her crowds going. "I wrote this song so I could live out my cheerleader fantasy!" she said in a press release. "I just wanted to make something simple and silly that I could do with the audience because I'm a huge fan of audience participation. Also, [I] selfishly (and shamelessly) wanted to bounce around on stage singing a song about being hot." It's this confident honesty that make Chappell one of the most exciting—and subversive—pop stars we've seen in practically forever. ★

"H-O-T T-O G-O!" Chappell's video for this song showcases her effervescence, while giving fans (and her sweet grandparents, who make a cameo) an easy-to-follow arm routine akin to "Y.M.C.A." Released August 11, 2023, the video was shot in Springfield, Missouri (a couple of miles from her hometown of Willard). Aspects of Americana—from a diner to a mini golf course—highlight Chappell's humble beginnings, while the addition of stadium shots underscore just how big she's become. The "Hot to Go!" dance turned into a festival staple, with videos from her sets going viral due to the sheer volume of the crowd dancing along. In a behind-the-scenes look at the making of the video, Chappell revealed that she sings the song slightly differently during each performance because "I never know the lyrics."

On October 14, 2023, Chappell performed to a sold-out crowd of more than 2,000 at The Fillmore in Philadelphia.

FROM SMALL-TOWN SINGER TO *Superstar*

by Ilana Kaplan
music and culture writer

CHAPPELL'S beginnings were predominantly antithetical to her glittery, drag persona. Before she was "Chappell Roan," she was Kayleigh Amstutz, who grew up in Willard, Missouri, a conservative, small town in the middle of the Ozarks where, according to an interview with *The Guardian*, she attended church three times a week. "I grew up thinking being gay was bad and a sin," she told the outlet. At 12, little Kayleigh began playing the piano. At 14, she sang in public for the first time at her middle-school talent show, which she won. By 15, Chappell had written her first song: a "boring ballad" about a Mormon boy she had a crush on.

SACRIFICING FOR HER ART

In 2014, while attending a summer arts camp at age 16, she penned what would be the song that launched her career: a bittersweet, Lorde-esque ballad. After she shared "Die Young" (along with some covers) on YouTube, her music piqued the interest of label execs. In 2015, it seemed as if her dreams had come true when she signed with Atlantic Records. That's when Chappell Roan was born—a stage name dedicated to her late grandfather Dennis K. Chappell and his favorite song, Curley Fletcher's "The Strawberry Roan." But that early version of Roan wouldn't be recognizable to the millions of fans sporting cowboy and circus chic ensembles at her shows today. The early Chappell embraced a folk-pop sound.

The excitement of signing to a label came with a harsh reality for Chappell—missing out on life events like school, prom, and graduation. She commuted back and forth between Missouri and Los Angeles for two years, toiling away at her artistic development. "I was 17 and I thought I was gonna win a Grammy," she told *The Guardian*. "It's funny, because, when you sign to a label, that's when the real work begins."

A SOUND OF HER OWN

Chappell wasn't entirely invested in her folk-pop music's direction—she craved something bolder. She was "sick of singing and performing depressing songs," her then-producer Nick Bobetsky told *Rolling Stone*. An introduction to writer-producer Dan Nigro helped her reinvigorate and reinvent her sound. Over two days in 2018, Chappell and Nigro wrote the song that would kick-start her career—"Pink Pony Club"— a queer liberation anthem penned after her first trip to a gay club. "It was so impactful, like magic," she told *The Guardian* of that night. "It was the opposite of everything I was taught." The accompanying music video unveiled Chappell's campier, rhinestone cowgirl aesthetic.

Though Chappell and Nigro were ecstatic about the song, Atlantic Records wasn't impressed by it and urged her not to share it, prompting her to "second-guess" herself, she told *Rolling Stone*. In 2020, the label finally decided to release it, and fans and critics responded positively. However, during the

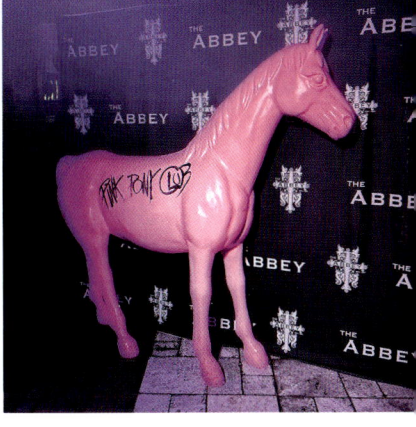

A night at The Abbey, a gay bar in West Hollywood, California, inspired "Pink Pony Club." Though the venue didn't have a pony back when Chappell first visited, it does now! The "pink" nods to a strip bar painted the color in Springfield, Missouri.

pandicmic, Chappell was dropped by the label, endured a breakup with her partner of more than four years, and struggled with her mental health. (In 2022, she revealed on Instagram that she has bipolar II, a mood disorder which can cause cycles of highs and lows. At the time, she told fans that it affected her "daily" and that she had received treatment in "intensive" outpatient therapy and individual therapy.)

During the pandemic, struggling in both her personal and professional life, she moved back to Missouri. Chappell even thought she might leave music altogether. "I was working the drive-through, and I was like, 'Oh my God, I think I'm just going to go to school' because I really wanted to be…I still want to be an art therapist where I go into schools and do art through craft therapy,'" she told *People*.

GIVING L.A. ANOTHER TRY

By the fall of 2020, she had returned to Los Angeles with the promise that she'd give the whole music career thing another year. There, she took on a handful of odd jobs, including nannying and serving as a personal assistant. "I worked at a donut shop for most of the time," Chappell told *People*, referencing Donut Friend, a plant-based donut shop in L.A., where she would hang out and eat donuts with Olivia Rodrigo, who also worked with Nigro.

When the one-year mark of her return to L.A. came around, Chappell's luck began to change. She reconnected with Nigro, continued developing her sound while embracing a campier aesthetic, and by 2022, she had signed a publishing deal with Sony. As an independent artist, she began writing and sharing tracks that felt authentic to her vision—like "Naked in Manhattan" and "My Kink Is My Karma"—and gained a following on TikTok as she quipped about the music industry and her dating experiences.

At the same time, "Pink Pony Club" was reaching a new audience through the powers of social media, and Rodrigo asked Chappell to open the San Francisco show on her Sour Tour in May 2022. As her fan base grew, other music labels began to show interest in her. However, Chappell refused to compromise the freedom she'd developed as an independent

A fresh-faced Chappell performed at The Showbox in Seattle on September 30, 2017. The 19-year-old was a supporting act for Vance Joy ("Riptide") during a U.S. leg of his Lay It On Me Tour. She performed her early songs "Meantime," "Bitter," and "Bad for You." It was her first time on the road, and fans were ready to cheer her on. "As I was walking out on stage, they were screaming for me, and that had never happened for me before," she told Set list.fm at the time. Chappell shared with *Unclear Magazine* in December 2017 that her first touring experience was "a whirlwind."

During the last stop of her debut tour, Naked In North America on March 15, 2023, Chappell shined on The Fonda Theatre stage in Los Angeles. On the 20-date tour, she performed "Femininomenon," "Red Wine Supernova," and "Hot to Go!" as well as a cover of Alanis Morissette's "You Oughta Know." Each stop featured a themed dress code that Chappell encouraged fans to abide by: Phoenix fans had a "Pink Pony" theme, while Portland, Oregon's assigned look was "Homecoming Queen." During each stop, in lieu of musical guests, Chappell highlighted local drag performers as her opening acts, championing the community that allows her art to thrive. "What's the point in making a pop project where your main audience is queer if you're not giving back?" she asked *DIY* magazine in 2023.

artist. "I was like, 'Give me a [pitch] deck on how you would market me. Give me a deck on what you would do with my career. What do you see in five years?'" she told *Rolling Stone*.

BREAKING THROUGH!

During her one-month debut tour as an independent artist, Naked in North America, which kicked off in Phoenix' Crescent Ballroom in February 2023, Chappell further cultivated her glam-pop onstage aesthetic. By March 2023, she signed with Nigro's Amusement Records, a partnership with Island Records. After years of chipping away at pop stardom, she had her breakthrough with the September 2023 release of her debut album, *The Rise and Fall of a Midwest Princess*. Critics and fans praised the songs—and they took on a whole other life when she started performing them live during her Midwest Princess Tour, which kicked off September 20, 2023, at the Gillioz Theatre in Springfield, Missouri.

The fandom for Chappell's drag persona and glittery-pop anthems steadily increased, helped by her March 2024 NPR Tiny Desk concert and her presence on TikTok. Her popularity exploded in April 2024 when she released the comphet kiss-off "Good Luck, Babe!" as a standalone single. (Comphet, short for "compulsory heterosexuality," is the theory that people are socially conditioned to behave as if they're straight regardless of their actual orientation.) "Good Luck, Babe!" topped the Billboard Pop Airplay chart and later became Chappell's first song to surpass one billion streams on Spotify. In April 2024, when she took the stage at Coachella for the second time and legendarily announced, "I'm your favorite artist's favorite artist," her fanbase suddenly swelled even more.

In June 2024, Chappell created what *Rolling Stone* described as "pure pop euphoria" at Governors Ball in New York City, proving her Coachella performance wasn't a fluke. Cosplaying as the Statue of Liberty, she used her platform to highlight the importance of what "freedom" means to her, starting by reciting some of the words inscribed on the pedestal of the Statue of Liberty: "Give me your tired, your poor, your huddled masses yearning to breathe free." Chappell added, "That means freedom in trans rights, that means freedom

Chappell took her talents to the Tiny Desk. The commanding performer headed to Washington, D.C., for NPR's online concert series, where both established mainstream acts and bubbling underground musicians hold intimate, often-stripped-down sets befitting the small office's tight space. During her 23-minute concert, Chappell sang five songs ("Casual," "Pink Pony Club," "Picture You," "California," "Red Wine Supernova") and was accompanied by a makeup-smudged, seven-piece band. The performance was bolstered by Chappell's theatrical, drag-inspired prom queen look (which she ranks as her third favorite of 2024 on Instagram), complete with a silver tiara and frilly dress. As of March 2025, her Tiny Desk concert has garnered more than 14 million views on YouTube.

Welcome to the U.S. of Chappell! On June 9, 2024, the star took a hit at New York City's Governors Ball Music Festival. Removing the body paint required bathing in dish soap, she told Alex Cooper on *Call Her Daddy*.

in women's rights…and it especially means freedom for all oppressed people in occupied territories." The crowd roared.

Chappell's huge draw at Governors Ball prompted her to land larger stages at Bonnaroo Music & Arts Festival in Tennessee and Lollapalooza in Chicago. By September 2024, Chappell had won the award for Best New Artist at the MTV Video Music Awards, where she dedicated her win to the queer and trans community. She made her *Saturday Night Live* debut in November, introducing her then unreleased track "The Giver."

STAYING TRUE TO HERSELF

After years of highs and lows for Chappell, it was satisfying to watch her take home her first Grammy in February 2025 for Best New Artist. Hers was a hard-won victory after plenty of artistic setbacks and a testament to being authentic to oneself despite music industry naysayers. It was at this pinnacle that Chappell's used her acceptance speech to advocate for the artists who now struggle as she had: "I told myself if I ever won a Grammy and I got to stand up here in front of the most powerful people in music, I would demand that labels and the industry profiting millions of dollars off of artists would offer a livable wage." Chappell never abandoned her roots—or forgot about the basic resources she could have used when she was trying to make it in Los Angeles. By pushing the music industry to be more supportive of the artists following in her footsteps, she's shown herself as a daring role model. After all, taking action to make life better for those who come after you is one of the truest markers of success.

Chappell is now one of the most famous artists in the world as a Grammy winner with 43.6 million monthly Spotify listeners, two BRIT Awards, and a Billboard Music Award. Her debut album peaked at No. 2 on the Billboard 200 chart. But beyond her heartwarming success, Chappell has reminded music fans of what makes a star: irreverent pop hits, a touch of sparkle, a sense of humor, a platform for advocacy, and a tight-knit community. And she's just beginning. As Chappell herself posted on X in December 2024, "The best way I know to express myself is through music, so hold on to your hats— there is more to come. ★

Wearing a runway-ready Acne Studios frock and a yellow medieval-style hennin (or coned headdress), Chappell accepted the award for Best New Artist at the 2025 Grammy Awards. She used her acceptance speech to advocate for music-industry change, like providing health insurance for artists. She hugged longtime creative director, Ramisha Sattar, before accepting her award. Sattar, who was Chappell's date to the event, later wrote on Instagram: "watching you grow as a human and an artist every day is so so special, and to see the world celebrating you is everything and more."

Chappell performed "My Kink Is Karma" at GLAAD's "Beyond" Spirit Day Concert in Los Angeles on October 19, 2022. The celebratory night of music hosted by Justin Tranter—which featured acts like Billy Porter and Dan Reynolds of Imagine Dragons—served as a fundraiser to support GLAAD's mission of empowering and protecting LGBTQ youth, a cause Chappell continues to champion. The fourth annual event raised $400,000 toward that goal. Tranter co-wrote "My Kink is My Karma" and would go on to help pen the Grammy-nominated "Good Luck, Babe!" In a 2024 interview with *InStyle*, he referred to Chappell as a "brilliant woman."

Chappell attended Universal Music Group's Grammy Awards after-party on February 5, 2023, at Milk Studios in Los Angeles. Two years later, she was nominated for six awards at the 67th Annual Grammys, including Album of the Year (*The Rise and Fall of a Midwest Princess*) and Record of the Year and Song of the Year (both for "Good Luck, Babe!").

Fans filled the House of Blues during the Chicago stop of The Midwest Princess Tour on October 5, 2023. Chappell's sophomore tour was named after her self-proclaimed moniker. "It's important for me to capture the Midwestern aspect. I don't want to lose that part of me," the Missouri native told *Variety*. Though she played at large events (like Coachella and Governors Ball festival) during the later legs of the tour, Chappell favors more intimate locations. (House of Blues' maximum standing capacity is 1,800.) "Local venues just rock so much more than massive company buildings," she told *Jacksonville Music Experience* in 2023. "The smaller venues are much more fun to play. A lot more personal, you can see everyone in the room and really just get to know the staff more."

On November 9, 2023, Chappell turned Portland, Oregon's Wonder Ballroom into an "unshakable safe haven for liberated joy," according to independent publication *Local Wolves*.

At Wonder Ballroom in Portland, Oregon, on November 9, 2023, the audience followed Chappell's "Hot to Go!" moves. This stop on the Midwest Princess Tour came just a couple months after the highly anticipated release of *The Rise and Fall of a Midwest Princess*, which dropped September 22, 2023. The 14-track album was praised for its "bold and uproarious pop," by *Pitchfork*. "I rose from the ashes of losing all my money and moving back in with my parents and working the drive-through," Chappell told *Variety* of the rocky road to her album, upon its release. "This beautiful project came to life from the deep pits of hell."

Olivia Rodrigo pulled Chappell to the stage for a surprise duet of "Hot to Go!" at L.A.'s Intuit Dome on August 20, 2024. After a prior appearance on the Sour Tour, Chappell again served as her friend's opening act—this time for the first five weeks of the Guts World Tour. "I absolutely adore [Chappell]," an emotional Olivia told the massive crowd in L.A. "I think she is one of the most singular, inspiring, powerful artists I've ever had the pleasure of meeting." When speaking with *Time* about their relationship in 2024, Chappell noted that "[Olivia] handles her career with grace...she gives me really great advice about how no one has it figured out."

"We're going to teach you a dance!"

— Chappell on the Guts World Tour, 2024

Chappell, here with Olivia Rodrigo, was a serious cross-country runner in high school and loves intense cardio—both on and off the stage!

"There's a special place in my heart for queer kids in the Midwest because I know how they're feeling and I know how isolating it can feel."

—Chappell to *The Washington Post,* 2023

In one of her most blatant homages to drag, Chappell performed in a Divine-inspired getup for her headlining set at Louisville's Kentuckiana Pride on June 15, 2024. Divine was the stage persona of late actor and singer Harris Glenn Milstead, known for his energetic and "filthy" appearances on screen and stage. The festival was sold out for the first time in its 24-year history, likely due to Chappell's popularity.

Chappell's debut on one of the biggest stages at Bonnaroo Music & Arts Festival on June 16, 2024, in Manchester, Tennessee, was a major moment. Festival organizers made a last-minute stage switch to accommodate the anticipated crowd size for the star's 3 p.m. set. *The Tennessean* reported that some Chappell supporters even began camping out at 3:30 a.m. to claim their spots for her performance.

"I was at a park down the street from The Abbey when Chappell performed 'Pink Pony Club' for the first time. She was a vision in red, playing a keyboard on the stage of an amphitheater for a small crowd of queer women gathered to fundraise for a new lesbian bar. Her voice echoed to the top of the theater where I sat hashing out dyke drama with my ex's best friend. As women around us jumped up to clap to a song about finding the space to be free, my ex's friend and I picked up on the queer joy. We agreed the statute of limitations had passed and I could move on. It was the start of Chappell providing a Sapphic soundtrack to our lives. That lesbian bar never opened, but Chappell created a queer space we'd lacked. From one Midwest Princess to another, I'm gonna keep on dancing."

–Trish Bendix, culture writer

After canceling appearances at the All Things Go festival in New York and Columbia, Maryland, due to emotional struggles, Chappell returned to her Midwest Princess Tour on October 1, 2024. While performing for a sold-out crowd at FirstBank Amphitheater, in Franklin, Tennessee, she addressed the queer community. "I needed this so bad when I was 15. I felt so completely misunderstood and alone," she said. "You are cherished, and you are loved. I'm gonna say it again, because I have a feeling that sometimes it's hard to hear these things, or maybe you don't hear them at all. But if you're here, then you are loved and you are cherished."

"Thank you thank you thank you. I will remember this forever."

—Chappell on Instagram, 2024

For her set at Lollapalooza Music Festival in Chicago on August 1, 2024, Chappell sported white face paint and a trans flag–colored, Lucha libre–inspired outfit, designed by Zana Bayne. Chappell's set reportedly had the most attendees at a daytime performance in Lollapalooza history. To accommodate her massive crowd, Chappell swapped set times with Kesha. Chappell wrote on Instagram that she was moved to tears by the size of her audience: "I was crying as I walked on stage at @lollapalooza because of the overwhelm of support."

Nearly everyone at Lollapalooza in Chicago's Grant Park made a beeline for the T-Mobile stage for Chappell's 5 p.m. set on August 1, 2024. Halfway through her performance, she even did a full split!

The Midwest Princess Tour culminated with a final performance on October 13, 2024, during Austin City Limits Music Festival. Rachel Parker of the *Dallas Observer* noted that Chappell seemed relaxed during her Sunday set at Zilker Park. Above, Chappell is seen high-kicking and parading around the stage with electric energy. In total, she played 89 shows across the U.S., Canada, Europe, and Australia over the course of one year.

Her luchador mask off, Chappell revealed gleaming silver eye makeup at Lollapalooza on August 1, 2024, in Chicago's Grant Park.

Her Style
FANTASY, CAMP & QUEER JOY

LOOKING GOOD, FEELING *Gorgeous*

by Izzy Grinspan
digital director, *Harper's Bazaar*

EVERYONE has a favorite Chappell Roan look, whether she's wowing Coachella as a butterfly in tribute to Lady Miss Kier of Deee-Lite, dressed in homage to drag queen Divine at the Kentuckiana Pride festival, or as a feathered white swan on *The Tonight Show*. Whatever your prized Chappell getup, stylist Genesis Webb probably had a hand in creating it. "She brings the element of glam drag, and then I bring an element of more punk club kid," Webb explained to *Harper's Bazaar*.

Webb met Chappell at a *V* magazine shoot, where the two bonded over being from the Midwest and growing up far outside the industry. "Coming from more lower-class backgrounds, it just kind of brings this sense of familiarity in a space like that. And she's also such a girl's girl, and I was one of the only girls on the set," the stylist said. But what really stood out for Webb was Chappell's clarity of vision. "I'd worked with a couple people prior who were way bigger than her and who didn't really have a lot of opinions. But she had this really specific thing that she wanted to do."

That specific thing pays tribute to drag queens, pageant queens, horror movies, and pop divas. It wasn't Webb's personal aesthetic, which skews to the darker side: She's more likely to wear black and bleach her brows. The first thing you notice is the tattoo of the rosary inked up her neck, which she got to ensure that she would never "work a normal job." But she vibed with Chappell's appreciation for what she calls "Midwest trashy glam," and the singer admired the racks of vintage Webb brought on set.

As Chappell's stylist, Webb's fashion influences are informed and thoughtful. She pulls from twisted old films like John Waters' 1972 filth extravaganza *Pink Flamingos* (tagline: "An exercise in poor taste") and the 2003 club-kid-murderer drama *Party Monster*. At one point, she referenced an Elton John look

Chappell (nude pantyhose crowning her head) and stylist Genesis Webb went Victorian Gothic, in keeping with the Alexander McQueen show during Paris Fashion Week on March 8, 2025. The late great designer is a favorite of Webb's. "I watch his shows to this day, and I've seen them a million times, but I literally shed a tear because of how beautiful it is," she told *Harper's Bazaar.*

from 1980. She describes herself as "anti-fashion," but worships at the antlered altar of the late visionary Alexander McQueen, known for his subversive and memorable designs. "I love Rick Owens and Yohji Yamamoto, that very dark and long silhouette," Webb says. "I like a lot of black, but then there are designers who have recently taken over my brain, like Viktor & Rolf or Thom Browne. I love that Chappell World is opening me up to, like, 'Oh, we can do a little color, we can add more, take more risks.' And I've just gained a huge appreciation for the campy theatrical aspect not being so dark."

Webb's breadth of pop culture references came from Tumblr, her escape when she was coming of age in Oklahoma City and feeling alienated from everyone around her. "Anything weird, I just wanted to suck it up because I was in a space that did not allow a lot of that. Tumblr was so valuable," Webb says. "It introduced me to things like *Party Monster* or *Kids*, Harmony Korine." Kids today, Webb points out, are absorbing pop culture at a more frenetic pace than she was a decade ago. "It's like you can barely keep up with what's being put out, so why would these kids try to find [things] from the past? I like bringing the references for the kids [in Chappell's outfits], so they can be like, 'Who the fuck is this? Who's Divine?'"

But if Chappell's concert experience is for the kids, it's also for, well, everybody else. "She cultivates such a huge queer space—obviously, having drag queens open—and it's just such an amazing and safe experience," Webb says. "And then I think just adding on the '90s, '80s, also queer references to bring it all together just works really well, and gives it the ability to jump across generations." On TikTok, fans have rallied around a video of a white-haired older man belting out Chappell's hit "Pink Pony Club" from the balcony at a show. Webb says he's the uncle of Chappell's drummer, but the point remains: Chappell has created a space for the 26-year-olds and the Pink Pony Pawpaws.

Webb is aware that the fans are reading into every look, searching for hidden meanings. "It's crazy," she says. "We have to do more. People really think we're doing the Muppets. I love it. It's funny." So is it true she's based Chappell's looks on iconic Miss Piggy moments, as the meme suggests? She laughs: "On the record? It's just divine intervention." 🔥

LOOK HERE!

Chappell's stylist, Genesis Webb, breaks down four outfits we'll never forget.

BY IZZY GRINSPAN

BOSTON CALLING
Boston •
May 26, 2024

"The reference was this old cowgirl leotard that I've had saved since even before working with her. Zana Bayne made it; she's just such an amazing artist. Lacey Dalimonte made the custom coat, with trinkets on the collar that are customized for her. It even has a little Divine trinket."

GOVERNORS BALL
NYC • June 9, 2024

"That one was super collaborative. I sent Chappell a reference of a Playboy Bunny coming out of a cake, and she was like, 'Let's do an apple. We should have it be a bong, a smoking apple.' The Statue of Liberty came naturally. It's so camp and obviously, so New York, and Elton John's done it. And I had saved that Monique Fei dress for a long time, because of the butt opening. She's so game. She wants to do everything. I even made attachments for the belt, because I thought she might not want her butt out. And she was like, 'Can we take these off?'"

KENTUCKIANA PRIDE
Louisville, KY • June 15, 2024

"Our makeup artist, Andrew [Dahling], he's from Kentucky and he's a club kid; his looks are insane. So for him to do the Divine look in Kentucky, it all made sense. And then at the bridge of 'Casual,' these fireworks just went off. It was for a baseball game or something. It was just serendipity. But like a lot of the trajectory we've had, it felt like it was meant to be happening."

**BONNAROO
Manchester, TN •
June 16, 2024**
"This really amazing
latex company,
Aimless Gallery,
reached out to me and
wanted to do full looks
for everyone, for
nothing, just because
of their belief in us.
I had wanted to do the
Party Monster nurse
look for Halloween
for so long. It was just
a really sick queer
reference that I feel
like people who are
younger haven't seen.
I went to Bonnaroo
in 2014, when I was
16, and I was showing
everyone that movie.
So to be back in the
same place, seeing
those looks, it
brought it full circle.
I was crying the
whole time."

CHAPPELL'S FASHION INSPO

As Chappell's stylist, Genesis Webb pulls from cult movies, nostalgia, Americana, historic heroines, and more—then adds her own twist.

The Sisters of Perpetual Indulgence

beauty pageants

Playboy Bunnies

Party Monster

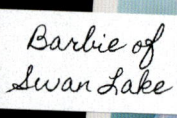

Barbie of Swan Lake

56

Divine

Julie d'Aubigny

early 1980s
Elton John

McQueen's
2009 show
"Horn of
Plenty"

Miss Piggy

WORK IT, *Girl!*

by J'na Jefferson
music and culture journalist

DRAG as an art form goes way back—dating back to the dawn of theater in Ancient Greece. However, the growing visibility of drag over recent decades—in film, on screen, and on stage—has given today's queer artists, including Doechii and Troye Sivan, the freedom to weave its influence into their music. Chappell, who describes herself as a "singer/songwriter/performer/drag queen," occupies a unique space as both a wildly successful pop star and a purveyor of drag's spirit. Her music, aesthetic, and outspoken nature are deeply drag-infused, as she uses her platform to entertain, inspire, and amplify marginalized voices. Her elevation of this once-underground culture is also reshaping the queer direction of 21st-century pop music.

"I've always noticed when someone is using drag as a prop versus drag as a castmate," Hanukah Lewinsky, a drag performer in New York City, explains of Chappell's appreciation for the drag community, which has been proudly reciprocated. "There have been artists [in the past] who have had drag queens on stage, and [the queens] haven't been paid, they don't get tagged, they don't get any recognition."

"When Chappell has drag queens with her," Lewinsky adds, "it's 'this is so-and-so, this is where you can find their art, this is where you can find what they do.' We're her co-stars."

Lewinsky is among the performers who replaced Chappell at the 2024 All Things Go music festival after Chappell pulled out of her set for health reasons. The last-minute set, dubbed "Queens of the Dancefloor" by festival coordinators, was curated by NYC-based drag star Beaujangless the night before the event, and included several drag performers, including legendary queen Kevin Aviance, festive background dancers, and DJ B-Roc of The Knocks.

"Drag queens are used to getting something ready that's very exciting, very quickly," Lewinsky said. The queens stood in for the singer, lip-synching and dancing to a slew of Chappell songs for about 45 minutes. "The crowd really loved it—in that moment and online. The general consensus felt like we were able to add something exciting and new to that day," she explains.

"It was by far the coolest experience of my life thus far. Just that I got to do it to music that I love, for an artist that I love, with such close friends, it was 10/10. I wouldn't change it for the world," Lewinsky says.

THE IMPACT OF DRAG

Though Chappell's music reflects her queerness and affinity for drag, drag's influence on the music industry isn't new. In the 1930s, "Pansy" performer Jean Malin recorded songs referencing queer identity; while in the '50s, rock pioneer (and former drag queen) Little Richard's flamboyant stage persona paved the way for future LGBTQ+ performers. David Bowie's experimental sound, costumes, and theatrics were key in pivoting pop in a queer direction. Elton John's "lifelong love affair" with drag and a friendship with Divine encouraged the

Hanukah Lewinsky and other queens stood in for the artist at the 2024 All Things Go music festival at Forest Hills Stadium in New York City, while Chappell focused on her mental health.

Rocket Man's over-the-top costumes. In the 2010s, rapper Nicki Minaj embraced drag elements, notably with her alter ego "Roman Zolanski," which toyed with gender norms. Chappell is continuing a tradition set in motion long before her reign.

"Pop and rock specifically have always been informed by queer culture, and drag is also part of that conversation," explains Elyssa Maxx Goodman, the author of *Glitter and Concrete: A Cultural History of Drag in New York City*. "[Chappell's rise] has the possibility of continuing drag's presence in mainstream culture."

CHAPPELL'S USE OF DRAG

Chappell's discography is a proclamation of her queer identity, using drag-inspired themes to amplify self-discovery, empowerment, and resistance. "Pink Pony Club" celebrates queerness while exploring somberness, creating a drag-evoking emotional juxtaposition. "Femininomenon" flips the script, proudly embracing queer sexuality. She blends pop with elements of country, alt-rock, and folk (at times in the same song) mirroring how drag fuses high art with low culture. This art form has long challenged boundaries, not only of gender but also of music, bringing power to Chappell's work.

Pop has often used drag to create visual spectacles rooted in queer resistance and celebration. Through bold, avant-garde makeup and costumes—like her signature white face paint, a nod to her hometown's homophobes who called queer kids "clowns"—Chappell is helping to normalize drag's aesthetics. "The people in my hometown would call gay people 'clowns.' That's why I actually wear white face [drag makeup], because of how those people called us clowns. I was like, 'Bitch I'll show you a clown,'" she said to an audience in Manchester.

Goodman notes that Chappell highlights femme drag, a style in which women or nonbinary people dress in drag, popularized by performers like Fauxnique and Crimson Kitty. Chappell's drag-heavy aesthetic in her music videos and live performances adds to her allure. In the "My Kink Is Karma" video, she plays a lingerie-clad devil/clown, a nod to the apparently queer character HIM from *The Powerpuff Girls*. She also frequently uses blue eyeshadow, a deliberate tribute to the

Chappell and drag icon Sasha Colby have embraced each other in the media. In fact, Chappell's slogan "your favorite artist's favorite artist" is pulled from a comment Sasha made about herself during the "Meet the Queens" teaser video from season 15 of *RuPaul's Drag Race*. Chappell brought Sasha on stage to perform at the Capitol Hill Block Party in Seattle on July 19, 2024. Then, on September 11, 2024, Sasha introduced Chappell for her MTV VMAs debut, lovingly calling her "my daughter." "She's not a nepo baby—she's just talented, and she didn't have to use or barter her talent," Colby told *Harper's Bazaar* of her appreciation for Chappell. "She doesn't have to hide her sexuality, or hide anything. The songs are great. The writing is great. Her voice is insane."

Chappell (just 5'2") met the towering stars of *Drag: The Musical* at New World Stages on April 6, 2025, in New York City. The show was co-written by *RuPaul's Drag Race All Stars* winner Alaska Thunderfuck (far left).

sex workers and drag queens who have been unfairly demonized. As Chappell put it in *Faces of Music*, a documentary series sponsored by Sephora: "Blue eyeshadow is so stigmatized… and it's all connected to why I picked it."

"Drag and drag aesthetics have long been part of how pop musicians visually connect to their audiences," Goodman says, referencing Cher's Bob Mackie costumes, Madonna's Marie Antoinette–inspired outfit at the 1990 MTV VMAs, and Lady Gaga's early career looks, including her 2011 drag king persona "Jo Calderone."

Chappell's stage presence is bold and playful, drawing from drag's performative theatrics where every move tells a story. This allows her to explore both lighthearted and darker themes, reflecting drag's ability to blend cheek and earnestness. And the artist uses her live performances to advocate for LGBTQ+ rights and visibility. At the 2024 Governors Ball Music Festival, Chappell called for "freedom for all oppressed people" while dressed as the Statue of Liberty. A week later, at the Kentuckiana Pride celebration, she performed in full drag, paying tribute to legendary queen Divine's iconic role in the 1972 film *Pink Flamingos*.

STANDING UP FOR DRAG

"I feel like any time [Chappell has] a big platform, she lets people know that drag is here to stay," New York City queen Mo'Riah says about Chappell's commitment to drag. Like Lewinsky, Mo'Riah was one of the performers asked to dance in Chappell's place at All Things Go, a moment she says made her "feel like Beyoncé," adding that Chappell "always stands up for [drag queens.]"

"[Chappell's] touchstone comes at a time where there's a very odd turn back to 'We don't want anything that's out of line,'" Lewinsky notes of the tepid climate in which Chappell is finding her success, where queer and trans rights hang in the balance and are even under direct attack. "It would be so easy for someone to fit into what society deems appropriate, but it's nice to have someone who says, 'Fuck that, we're not going to tailor ourselves for what you deem is right or acceptable.' It's very energizing."

Lewinsky, who uses she/her pronouns while in drag, also performed during the New York stop of Chappell's Midwest

Designer Bob Mackie and Cher stepped out in elegance at the Costume Institute Gala at the Metropolitan Museum of Art in New York City in 1985.

Princess Tour. Chappell supported local drag acts by having them open for her during these shows, sharing the spotlight with performers who've been an integral part of her artistic journey.

"The first time I ever saw Chappell is when she came to one of my weekly gigs at Pieces," a popular West Village gay bar, Mo'Riah adds. "She even stayed after and watched the other show after ours. It's clear she loves drag, and she loves the community and the art of it. I think that's beautiful."

Unlike artists who may incorporate drag aesthetics without nourishing deeper ties to the community, Chappell's integration feels genuine. She's part of a wave of queer artists who aren't just referencing drag—they're making it a core part of their artistic DNA. Her drag persona is theatrical, but it's also authentic.

"[Drag] just feels like freedom," Chappell says in Sephora's *Faces of Music*. "It lights up something in my brain, it's just pure serotonin." ◊

Drag performer Plane Jane, dressed as the Pink Pony princess, attended the MTV Video Music Awards on September 11, 2024. Mirage Amuro trailed behind.

Veronica Pop (left) opened for Chappell at Chicago's House of Blues on October 5, 2023, during the Midwest Princess Tour. Chappell began the tradition of featuring drag queens as openers during her Naked in North America Tour, inviting local performers to submit via her X page for a chance to join the lineup.

"It's wonderful to see so many beautiful queer people here," drag artist Donna Trump (right) told the crowd at Manchester Academy in the U.K. on September 13, 2024. The show marked the first stop on the second European leg of the Midwest Princess Tour, with Donna Trump joining two other local acts to open for Chappell. She performed lip-synched renditions of Sabrina Carpenter's "Taste," as well as "Nobody's Perfect" and "The Best of Both Worlds," both by Hannah Montana (a.k.a. Miley Cyrus).

"When I say I was crying, I was on the floor crying," U.K.-based drag artist Tequila Thirst told *Curiously Media* of her experience opening for Chappell during the Manchester, England, stop of the Midwest Princess Tour on September 13, 2024. Tequila performed a medley from stars like Britney Spears, Katy Perry, and Lady Gaga. She also got a shout-out from Chappell in a speech championing drag, in which Chappell explained it's her "favorite thing to see drag embraced all over the world."

A BRIEF HISTORY OF DRAG

This art form has evolved over several centuries. BY J'NA JEFFERSON

Drag dates back to the beginning of theater itself. In Ancient Greece, only men were allowed to act, which led to them performing both male and female roles. In 17th-century Japan, men took over the originally all-female kabuki theater; authorities claimed it was rife with sex workers. Women generally weren't allowed to perform on Western European stages either. This gender exclusion eventually fueled cross-dressing outside the theater. It evolved into modern drag, so named in the 19th century because male performers wore female costumes such as gowns, which dragged on stage.

Julian Eltinge (right), a prominent drag performer of the early 20th century, was friends with Mary Pickford, an actress known as the "Queen of the Movies" at the time.

By the 20th century, drag had become a staple in vaudeville and variety theaters. According to Elyssa Maxx Goodman, author of *Glitter and Concrete: A Cultural History of Drag in New York City*, drag had to become palatable to straight club owners and audiences to succeed after the Prohibition Era, so the performers—known as "Pansies" in the 20s and 30s—adopted a subtler feminine look. However, after the 1969 Stonewall Uprising, people favored bold self-expression. Drag has evolved into a form of resistance that championed LGBTQ+ rights.

In recent decades, stars like Freddie Mercury and Boy George have brought drag mainstream. Icons like Lady Bunny, Dorian Corey, and Joan Jett Blakk have inspired joy, laughter, and change. The success of *RuPaul's Drag Race* as well as drama *Pose* have boosted drag's visibility, introducing a new wave of superstars.

This little piggy went "wee, wee, wee" all the way to Universal Music Group's 2024 Grammy Awards after-party. Chappell (left) sported a prosthetic pig nose and an escoffion, a two-horned headpiece worn by women in the late Middle Ages. Tyler Green, a Connecticut designer who created the nose, told *CT Insider* that seeing the design on Chappell was a "pinch me" moment. The look became iconic when Chappell used it for her "Good Luck, Babe!" single imagery.

Chappell (right) wore a vintage Scott McClintock dress and hooves from Etsy shop Creature Cosplay at the Spotify Best New Artist Party on February 1, 2024, in Los Angeles. The white face paint was a reference to the homophobes in her hometown, who called queer kids "clowns." "My biggest regret in life is that I gave up a full-ride scholarship to an arts high school called Interlochen," she told *Interview* in 2024. "It just would've been sick to save myself from a lot of queer violence. But at the same time, I would not be the Midwest Princess I am today if I had been around art kids. I look at my life and I'm like, 'Everything was exactly as it should have been.'"

> ## "I honored my inner child, and that's when my art got better."
>
> —Chappell to *Capital Buzz*, 2024

The pop star invited us into her glittery fantasy world with a performance of "Red Wine Supernova" on *The Late Show with Stephen Colbert* on February 15, 2024. Chappell descended onto the stage on a giant heart, while wearing vintage lingerie sourced from L.A.'s Palace Costume and bows designed by Mexican artist Moños de Mi Niñez (which means "Bows of My Childhood"). Genesis Webb told *Vulture* that the entire look was inspired by the brothel scene in the Oscar-winning film *Poor Things*. "All of the girls come out and they're very stylized in these lingerie-looking outfits," Chappell's stylist explained.

She came to *slay*. Chappell (left) donned a medieval-inspired look at the 2024 MTV VMAs. On the carpet, she channeled a queen in a tulle gown from Y/Project. Her makeup was more demure than usual, but still striking: Golden mascara and deep red lips enhanced her features and made her eye color pop. Her makeup artist for the night, Andrew Dahling, said the look was inspired by makeup icon Pat McGrath's work for Dior in the 2000s. "Dark romantic... very heavy on the eyes, very glowy skin, very ethereal," he told CNN. Chappell paired the look with a super-graphic ultra-sharp manicure, designed by Juan Alvear. Her nails were transformed into golden swords with two stacked layers of nail tips, according to *New Beauty*.

To accept her Moonman for Best New Artist (and first-ever major award), Chappell (right) slipped into a silver chainmail dress from Paco Rabanne. The outfit featured a matching headpiece and gloves and fit her medieval warrior motif for the night. "I dedicate this to all the drag artists who inspire me," she said to cheers. "And I dedicate this to queer and trans people who fuel pop."

For the 2025 Grammys red carpet, Chappell (left) donned a vintage 2003 Jean Paul Gaultier gown, featuring pale blue, goldenrod, and mustard tulle. Per *Harper's Bazaar*, the gown is quite literally a work of art—it features imagery from Edgar Degas' 1877 painting *Dancer with a Bouquet Bowing*. She completed the look with sheer blue fingerless gloves, John Fluevog lace-up boots, and a feathered hair accessory. Chappell later revealed to E! that she slept with the delicate couture gown, as she was "scared for its welfare."

Chappell's red carpet glam featured a blue and gold nail set (right) designed by Juan Alvear, bright, bold makeup, and an ombré headpiece. Her signature red curly hair cascaded elegantly down her back. According to Chappell's hairstylist Dom Forletta, texture was the goal. "Each product we chose to use was intentional to tie the entire look together and make her stand out on the carpet."

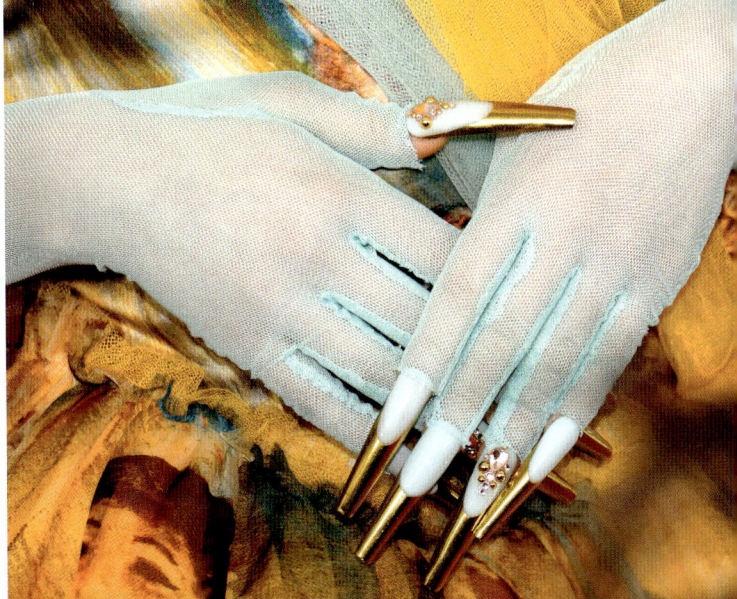

Thanks to the masterful hands of hairstylist Dom Forletta, Chappell's enviable ringlets were in pristine condition even after a long day of grabbing Grammy love. Forletta used a combination of curling irons as well as a figure-eight pinning method to give every strand a consistent pattern. "We've been working together for so long now, I really know her hair and its potential," he told *Fashionista*. "I've become more confident and experimental. ...I'm able to push boundaries and explore endless possibilities with her hair." Makeup artist Andrew Dahling created entirely different aesthetics for the red carpet and the ceremony— going from a striking yellow eyeshadow look to bold pink glam in a relatively short time. Eagle-eyed fans believe this was achieved through expert makeup layering, as pops of yellow could still be seen near Chappell's eyebrows.

"I was introduced to Chappell the same way I'm sure many straight, white, 40-something men were–by the cool younger woman at work. I'm not a regular at Pink Pony Clubs, and I'm more a '6/10 and sedentary' than 'Hot to Go,' but I have certainly been one of the 100 boys kissed in bars. What Chappell has done–through the power of breaking through–is to give guys like me insight into other cultures and experiences. This is the highest power of true art. Chappell speaks on non-universal truths. She sings the quiet parts out loud to us in the back. She's a troubadour of underrepresented audiences. The music she makes is undeniably necessary."

–Rocky Rakovic, writer and editor

A fashion trifecta for the ages, right here! Genesis Webb and Chappell sandwiched legendary fashion designer Betsey Johnson at the Daily Front Row's Fashion Los Angeles Awards on April 24, 2025, at the Beverly Hills Hotel. Chappell, with brushed out curls reminiscent of *Vogue*'s former creative director Grace Coddington, wore a dramatically peplumed Alexander McQueen dress from the fashion house's 2025–2026 Fall/Winter Collection. The night was a love fest for these three: Chappell presented the award for Music Stylist of the Year to Webb, and Johnson received a Lifetime Achievement Award. The iconic pink dress Chappell wore for the NPR Tiny Desk Concert was vintage Betsey Johnson, and Johnson told her TikTok fans she'd love to give Chappell the costumes that she wore as a teen."She's going to always surprise us," Johnson declared on TikTok before gushing about Chappell's styling, "It's perfect. It's perfect. Perfect."

To the surprise of no one, Chappell (left) devoured the red carpet during her first appearance at Paris Fashion Week in March 2025. Seen as a budding fashion icon, she wore a strapless metallic Rick Owens gown at the designer's show held at the Palais de Tokyo. "I always feel the coolest wearing Rick [Owens]," she told *Dazed*. Chappell's makeup embraced "weird and scary" beauty, complete with milky white contacts and black orbs symmetrically dotted on her face. "Anything weird, I just [want] to suck it up because I [grew up] in a space that did not allow a lot of that," she explained to *Harper's Bazaar* of her front-row look.

Chappell (right) served face while wearing a backless silver slip from Rabanne during the fashion house's Paris Fashion Week show on March 6, 2025. Her dramatic, drag-inspired eye makeup, painted by her master artist Andrew Dahling, brought spooky glamour to the stunning ensemble, which was styled by the one and only Genesis Webb.

Aside from her signature red tendrils, Chappell (left) was barely recognizable at the Alexander McQueen show during her first Paris Fashion Week. Seated front row on March 8, 2025, she wore a shirt with pointy lapels and a jacket with an exaggerated peplum, both from McQueen.

Let them eat cake! Chappell (right) stunned in a Marie-Antoinette–inspired dress by Valentino while attending the fashion house's show on March 9, 2025. The velvet bodice brings simplicity, while the bottom of the dress—an outrageous tulle ballgown skirt adorned with flower appliques—elevates its drama. She appeared almost cartoon-like with light pink foundation, pencil-thin eyebrows and spiked lower eyelashes. "I'm obsessed with the show, the collection, everything," Chappell wrote on Instagram about Valentino's latest collection, adding that she "[feels] like such a lucky girl" for being able to wear the brand's couture outfits.

"I'm very modest when it comes to my day-to-day... I used to dress fucking crazy... I would literally just wear my thong out, miniskirt, bottom ass cheeks out, nipples see through."

—Chappell on *Call Her Daddy*, 2025

In an act of sheer genius, Genesis Webb dressed Chappell in a twinkly jumpsuit over an ethereal top for the Vivienne Westwood Paris Fashion Week show on March 8, 2025. Makeup artist Andrew Dahling (the talent behind her Governors Ball Lady Liberty makeup, who is also from the Midwest) went wild with her eyes. "I love working with Chappell because she's so down for anything...she's not super picky, she's not afraid to get messy. She's not a celebrity that has to work a specific way," Dahling told *The Cincinnati Enquirer.* "We're all a bunch of misfits from the middle of nowhere with a crazy vision and crazy dream and so much talent."

On fashion's biggest night, Chappell didn't disappoint. At the Met Gala, held at New York City's Metropolitan Museum of Art on May 5, 2025, she wore a pink pantsuit with a stained-glass pattern (right) under a coat trimmed in sparkly fur (left). The ensemble leaned into the evening's dress code, "Tailored for You," reflecting the Met Costume Institute's spring exhibition, "Superfine: Tailoring Black Style."

Chappell sang "Hot to Go!" at the Outside Lands Festival at San Francisco's Golden Gate Park on August 11, 2024.

Her Sound
SEX, LOVE
& ABSOLUTE
BANGERS

THE *Spectacle* OF CHAPPELL

by Ilana Kaplan
music and culture writer

IN the trajectory of the world's biggest pop icons, certain astonishing moments raised the bar for all performers that followed: Madonna's brazenly sensual performance of "Express Yourself" in a John Paul Gaultier cone-bra corset during the 1990 Blond Ambition Tour. Lady Gaga's bloody demonstration of the perils of fame while performing "Paparazzi" at the 2009 MTV Video Music Awards. Beyoncé's history making, drumline-flanked headlining performance at Coachella in 2018. Taylor Swift's dive into the stage and graceful "underwater" swim, surfacing for the *Midnights* portion of her Eras Tour.

For Chappell Roan, that game-changing moment came in the summer of 2024 in New York City, when she broke through an apple bong dressed as a nearly naked Lady Liberty. From head-to-toe, she was drenched in the statue's particular shade of oxidized blue-green as she belted hits like "Pink Pony Club" and the location-appropriate "Naked in Manhattan." She used her appearance at the packed Governors Ball Music Festival to speak up for the rights of all oppressed people, the trans community, and women. On that day, through theater and spectacle, Chappell's star power became utterly undeniable.

Though the pandemic era teemed with whisper pop by singer-songwriters like Billie Eilish, Gracie Abrams, and Phoebe Bridgers, who soothed us during our many months of solitude, Chappell's ascent signaled a post-Covid shift to unapologetically loud, buoyant, catchy, pulsing anthems. This was music built for parties, clubs, crowds, and being out in the world in every way. Chappell emerged as a beacon of maximalism. No longer was the understated, introspective artist at the forefront of the music industry; instead, queerness, theatrical-pop, bold makeup, and (lots of) sequins were en vogue. Chappell reinvigorated pop music—and challenged the prevailing view of what a pop star

Chappell, as Lady Liberty, busted out of a Big Apple during her legendary performance at Governors Ball Music Festival in Flushing Meadows Corona Park in New York City on June 9, 2024.

"I am very introverted. I love being alone. I love playing video games by myself."

—Chappell to *Vanity Fair,* 2023

The Wonder Ballroom in Portland, Oregon, holds fewer than 800, so Chappell fans on the November 9, 2023, stop of her Midwest Princess Tour were treated to an intimate show—typical for this early period. "I never really expected [my career] to grow this big," she told *Interview* in 2024. "I feel like I peaked a couple of years ago. Back then, I was like, 'I sold out the Bowery Ballroom [capacity 600] and that's crazy.' It's been amazing to do bigger shows and open for Olivia [Rodrigo], but everything right now is truly icing on the cake."

looks like. In contrast to the stripped-down productions and subtle performances during the pandemic, Chappell doubled down on elaborate costumes, dramatic makeup, and a campy stage presence.

The pop star herself has said that her flamboyant on-stage character is just that—a character—which she has unshockingly compared to David Bowie's glam-rock alter ego Ziggy Stardust. Like Ziggy, Chappell uses her on-stage persona (and music) to express and explore sex, sexuality, and queer romance. On the Kate Bush–tinged comphet song "Good Luck, Babe!" she sings a kiss-off to a female ex who she believes will end up trapped in a marriage with a man; in the power ballad "Casual," she laments the pitfalls of a situationship with some NSFW lyrics about oral sex; on the glittery bomb "Naked in Manhattan," Chappell yearns to have a "cinematic" sex scene like the one in the 2001 film *Mulholland Drive*; and in the queer liberation anthem "Pink Pony Club," she celebrates being able to be comfortable in her own skin in Los Angeles.

Like Bowie, Chappell creates distinct worlds through music, making her songs a complete audio-visual experience. She weaves theatrical elements into both her songwriting and performance. Songs like "Pink Pony Club" and "My Kink Is Karma" aren't just pop tracks—they're fully realized character studies brought to life with distinct personas and storylines.

Bowie is just one of the larger-than-life pop icons who has influenced the artist. Chappell pays homage to *Purple Rain*–era Prince through her gender-bending ease, funky guitar riffs, '80s synth-pop influences, campy ensembles, and the high-energy drama she brings to her shows. Much like Prince's look, Chappell's style is rooted in the power of self-expression. Prince rebelled against gender norms and embraced androgyny— sporting leotards, ass-less pants, feathers, heels, and shimmery suits. He not only oozed sex, but also helped redefine masculinity, in the way the Chappell is redefining femininity.

"Prince made being who you are/were acceptable. Owning your sexuality, creativity, and being expressive regardless of what someone said or thought. He put a stamp on being yourself," radio host Joyce Littel told NBC News in April 2016. On stage, Chappell embraces an (at-times) hyper-sexualized

Prince performed during his Welcome 2 America Tour on February 7, 2011, at NYC's Madison Square Garden. The rocker played 36 songs, including four encores.

fantasy with big hair, white face makeup, vibrant eyeshadow, and costumes that range from horror-inspired to burlesque. Like the Purple One, Chappell refuses to be categorized.

Her success isn't a fleeting trend. The maximalist look Chappell has cultivated has permeated not only the music industry but also fashion, makeup, and broader aesthetics. Since Chappell's rise, we've seen Gaga return to the larger-than-life visuals that helped cement her as a star and Addison Rae harness the tacky Y2K sartorial edge of OG pop princesses like Britney Spears and Christina Aguilera. Chappell is not only a tastemaker, but she's also set the stage for what the future of theatrical pop can look like. And it's not going anywhere anytime soon. ♥

Chappell, clowns, and comrades commanded the 2025 Grammys, performing "Pink Pony Club," the very song she says Atlantic Records tried to discourage her from releasing years earlier. "It feels so good to prove them wrong, because they weren't just a little wrong—they were very, very, very wrong. To know that my gut was right is the best feeling in the world," she told *Rolling Stone* in 2024.

During Chappell's debut performance on the Which Stage at Bonnaroo Music & Arts Festival in Manchester, Tennessee, on June 16, 2024, she taught fans how to do the "Hot to Go!" dance, a simple routine that encourages crowd involvement and interaction, similar to "Y.M.C.A." Chappell also performed "Picture You" while serenading an ash-blond wig on a mic stand, which she named "Wigelita," a third of the way through her nearly hour-long set. Her look was an homage to Chloë Sevigny's nurse outfit from the 2003 film *Party Monster*, according to stylist Genesis Webb. The cult classic chronicles the real-life story of a Midwestern teen who moves to New York City, becomes a club promoter, and spirals into addiction and murder.

At the 2024 Kentuckiana Pride festival, Chappell paid tribute to two looks made legendary by Divine, the cult drag icon and frequent John Waters collaborator. Chappell wore a mermaid-style red dress (left) by Irish designer Oran O'Reilly—inspired by Divine's most notable role in 1972's *Pink Flamingos*. She then removed the dress to reveal a leopard bodysuit (above), nodding to *Female Trouble*. "I like to believe madame divine [sic] was watching over the performance and she was the one who set off the fireworks during 'Casual,'" Chappell wrote on Instagram. "Divine if you are reading this from heaven...come down and haunt me sometime." Chappell and her band were painted by her makeup artist, Andrew Dahling.

THE SOUND OF HER
OF HER
Voice

by Patrick Crowley
art director and pop music expert

EVERY year, a wave of rising stars emerges, but something about Chappell Roan's ascension into the pop culture zeitgeist feels different. She styles herself like a competitor on *RuPaul's Drag Race* while peers like Charli XCX and Olivia Rodrigo opt for a '90s mallrat aesthetic. She is deliciously outspoken in a celebrity culture that has been media-trained into near-total inauthenticity, and she's loudly and proudly lesbian while American politics swing drastically more conservative every day. Though these distinctions certainly make Chappell stand out, there's one aspect of her artistry that has been overlooked: her voice.

For the past decade, female vocals in pop music have softened. The baby-voiced coo, originally popularized by Gwen Stefani and Britney Spears, saw a major resurgence (think: Camila Cabello, Halsey, Selena Gomez) and has yet to fade. Seriously, we haven't had a bona fide breakout star with full-throated pipes since Ariana Grande dropped *Yours Truly* in 2013. No one is placing Chappell's vocal abilities on the same level as, say, Whitney Houston's gospel-infused, multi-octave range or Adele's rich, full-throated belt. But hearing a voice on the radio with a real punch behind it is incredibly refreshing.

It's not just the power of Chappell's pipes that make her voice so transcendent; she also has an incredible amount of control. Though she's not classically trained, she effortlessly flips between her full chest voice to her falsetto to essentially yodel in a way that evokes '90s heroines like k.d. lang, Sinéad O'Connor, Linda Perry, and Dolores O'Riordan. (Chappell's pitch-perfect live cover of The Cranberries' "Dreams" is required viewing!)

Chappell's meteoric rise will undoubtedly inspire the music industry to chase flamboyant, hyper-stylized pop stars in hopes of finding the next big thing. Let's hope executives have noticed the substance beneath her outrageous style and that there's a craving among audiences for big-voiced divas. It's Chappell's soaring soprano—not her candy-colored eyeshadow—that has compelled everyone from toddlers to festival crowds to Elton Freaking John to wail along to "Pink Pony Club." ♥

Chappell's powerful belt commanded a crowd of more than 40,000 at the Boston Calling Music Festival at Harvard Athletics Complex, along the Charles River, on May 26, 2024.

It's no surprise that Chappell found a fan in iconic singer-songwriter Sir Elton John—the trailblazing theatrical LGBTQ+ musician and activist. The two artists performed together at the Elton John AIDS Foundation's 33rd Annual Academy Awards Viewing Party on March 2, 2025. Their set included duets of "Pink Pony Club," as well as renditions of Sir Elton's "Your Song" and "Don't Let the Sun Go Down on Me." Though both acts are known for their extravagant stage costumes, they dialed back the drama for the night, with Chappell looking dapper in a velvet jacket and purple trousers, both from Valentino. "Not only is she an incredible talent, but she also uses her voice and platform to stand up for her beliefs," the Rocket Man wrote about Chappell on Instagram before the event, which raised more than $8.9 million for HIV prevention, education, and services.

Though pageant queen iconography is not entirely new when it comes to album covers, Chappell's use of the motif for *The Rise and Fall of a Midwest Princess* holds a deeper purpose both aesthetically and sonically. The album artwork, shot by Ryan Clemens, highlights her many facets, from semi-serious to goofy and unapologetic. With that rebellious spirit, Chappell challenges the rules and expectations of how a pop star "ought" to be, through her art. In her music, she builds a world that mirrors and transcends her reality. The fantasy she conveys isn't just about escaping: It's about taking control of her own story, pushing back against society's limits, and facing the messiness of life. Though Chappell is from a small town, she's clearly meant for bigger things. "The songs are kind of the fairy-tale version of what happened in real life," she told *Vanity Fair* in 2023. "A lot of the songs are just enhanced versions of what happened or maybe they never happened at all."

Heading into uncharted waters. Chappell's 2025 single, "The Giver," is her take on country music. Co-written by Dan Nigro and officially released on March 13, 2025, the track marked her first single since "Good Luck, Babe!" nearly a year earlier. The fiddle-heavy pop song features rock-tinged guitars, a kickin' drum, and infectious hook. ("Take it like a taker, 'cause baby I'm a giver," she sings on the lesbian-friendly chorus.) Though she's not a country artist by nature, Chappell's vocal twang is spot-on. "Right now I'm just making songs that make me feel happy and fun," she wrote on Instagram before the song's release, squashing rumors of officially diving into country. "May the classic country divas lead their genre, I am just here to twirl and do a little gay yodel for y'all." A series of cheeky, double entendre–filled ads rolled out ahead of the single's release, featuring Chappell "getting the job done" in a variety of roles—including a dentist, construction worker, plumber, and detective.

THE *Women* WHO PAVED THE WAY

---

by Ilana Kaplan
music and culture writer

FORTY years before Chappell took home the Grammy for Best New Artist, that award went to a girl from Queens: Cyndi "She's So Unusual" Lauper. And years before Lauper came on the scene, Dolly Parton, with her larger-than-life personality, tender Southern storytelling, and her own scrappy climb to success, earned her first Grammy Award.

Like Parton and Lauper, Chappell has thrived as a singular force in music—honing her own visual and sonic identity and rebelling against the mainstream by embracing theatricality, drag, inclusivity, and her unwavering political activism. What's been so appealing about Chappell is how she's a student of these women—and others. These five artists have helped shaped Chappell into the artist she is today.

DOLLY PARTON

In many ways, Chappell is like Dolly Parton's red-headed lesbian protégée. Both artists share a striking artistic DNA that is apparent in their music and visual identities and also in their activism. Like Parton, Chappell had a Christian, conservative upbringing (the former in Tennessee, the latter in Missouri), and despite her background (or perhaps because of it) became a beacon of unwavering self-expression.

Throughout Chappell's career, she has used Parton's maximalist blueprint and shaped it for a new era, paying homage to Parton's tacky but glamorous aesthetic—putting her own spin on the "rhinestone cowgirl" with her costume selections—and using heightened femininity and camp as artistic weapons. Both women have openly uplifted the queer community; while Parton has inspired drag queens around the world, Chappell has made them opening acts at her shows.

Beyond the visual nods, Chappell also draws musical influence from Parton. Chappell's single, "The Giver," which she debuted during her performance on *SNL* in November 2024, is a Sapphic banger that flaunts her country lilt and echoes Parton's spunkiness and biting storytelling. And though the songs have different plotlines, Parton's "9 to 5" seemingly laid the groundwork for the spirited rallying cry that carries Chappell's "Pink Pony Club."

KATE BUSH

It's near-impossible to pinpoint one quality that has made Chappell so magnetic, because she's created an entire visual and sonic universe that is just plain magical. Kate Bush, whom Chappell has cited as one of her biggest influences, created such a world before her. Both musicians have embraced vivid

Long before Chappell bedazzled her costumes, Dolly Parton more than twinkled at The Auditorium Theater in Chicago on November 2, 1977.

Kate Bush sang "Running Up That Hill" on German TV's *Peter's Pop Show* in 1985. She would go on to inspire a spectrum of artists.

storytelling imagery, theatrical performances, and a genre-fluid approach to their music (with Bush veering a bit more art rock at times).

Bush's influence on Chappell is perhaps most apparent on her '80s-tinged single "Good Luck, Babe!" a breezy but bittersweet synth-pop anthem that details her ex-lover's experience of comphet dooming their romance. On the track's chorus, Chappell's yodeling belt echoes the pleading chorus of Bush's seminal hit "Running Up That Hill (A Deal with God)." It's also reminiscent of her debut single, the melodramatic "Wuthering Heights." Much as Chappell faced resistance from her first label over "Pink Pony Club," Bush also encountered pushback: EMI initially wanted a different song than "Wuthering Heights" as her first single. Lucky for the world, both artists persisted—and proved the execs wrong.

STEVIE NICKS

What artists *haven't* bowed before Stevie Nicks, really. With her smoky vocals, witchy ethos, advocacy for women's rights, and affinity for flowy shawls, the Fleetwood Mac singer has long inspired top musicians including Harry Styles, Haim, and Miley Cyrus. Chappell counts herself as one of them. In a 2018 interview with *ANCHR Magazine*, she cited Nicks, who she would try to "mimic," as one of her "main vocal influences."

Chappell's histrionic belt on many of her hits evokes an '80s Nicks' on tracks like "Stand Back" and "Edge of Seventeen." Chappell also appears to take cues from Nicks' evisceration of Lindsey Buckingham on "Silver Springs" with her own kiss-off, "Good Luck, Babe!" Chappell has even paid homage to Nicks with covers of "Dreams" and "Landslide."

As Chappell has garnered more fame, Nicks has acknowledged her impact on the rising star—and praised her for taking care of her mental health. Of the music industry execs orchestrating Chappell's grueling schedule, Nicks told *Rolling Stone*, "I said, 'They'll burn her out if that's what they want to do, because there's always somebody to replace you.' It must make them all very fearful. That's why it's good that Chappell just said, 'Well, go ahead, replace me. I'm canceling because I'm not going to drop dead for all you people.'"

Stevie Nicks dreaminess was captured on July 19, 1978, at Alpine Valley Music Theatre in East Troy, Wisconsin.

SIOUXSIE SIOUX

As a hallmark of the '80s punk scene, Siouxsie Sioux of Siouxsie and the Banshees brought a fearless, dark, glamorous edge to the London club scene while sporting bondage-inspired attire. Chappell's affinity for dramatic eye makeup could have been lifted from the Banshees' "Happy House" music video. Similar to Sioux, whose impressive range reached piercing highs and raspy lows, Chappell's vocal abilities can't be boxed in. Dave Sitek of the band TV on the Radio put it simply, speaking about Sioux: "There is no one who sings like that." Except maybe Chappell? Fun fact: Back in 1980, Siouxsie and the Banshees released an album called *Kaleidoscope.* Coincidence?

Britain's Siouxsie Sioux, in 1979, looked every bit the epitome of an ultra modern punk rock dream girl.

CYNDI LAUPER

In the '80s, Cyndi Lauper's "true colors" were vibrant. With her teased, rainbow-hued hair, rebellious fashion sense, virtuoso vocals, which oscillated between Betty Boop–like to powerhouse, and advocacy for the LGBTQ+ community, Lauper became a pop icon who was admired for embracing her eccentricity. Chappell has seemingly taken a page out of Lauper's book when it comes to her look, sporting clashing prints and campy ensembles—not to mention her big copper curls—which add to the drama of her performances. Even Lauper couldn't help but share her admiration for Chappell's "performance art" (and note its similarities to her own) in a September 2024 episode of *Watch What Happens Live!* "It's visual, it's so visual," she said. "You know I love those visual things, obviously."

Cyndi Lauper, here at the Grammy Awards on February 28, 1984, also broke taboos. She co-wrote "She Bop" about female masturbation.

In two of their respective biggest hits, both artists call powerfully for liberation and celebration. Lauper's "Girls Just Want to Have Fun" (a feisty, feminist anthem that was originally a masculine punk song written by a man) emanated joy and became a rallying cry for gender equality. Chappell's "Pink Pony Club" is a disco-pop metaphor for finding queer joy, self-acceptance, and "wicked dreams" in a gay strip club. Deeper in Lauper's discography, the bouncy synth and chanty chorus of her chaotic "Yeah Yeah" make it a sonic cousin to "Hot to Go!" ♥

WHO DOES CHAPPELL LISTEN TO?

Your Favorite Artist can't pick just one Favorite Artist. BY PATRICK CROWLEY

RIHANNA

"I started writing music because I heard 'Stay' by Rihanna and I was like, 'How do I write that song?'" Chappell told BBC Radio. "That album shows a side to her that we don't see very often."

FEIST

"I think I listen to Feist's *Let It Die* album once a week, honestly, for the past two years," Chappell shared with *It's Real.* "It's just like my favorite comfort album."

SZA

Chappell named SZA as her dream collaborator on the *Call Her Daddy* podcast. SZA's response? "Actually [I] didn't believe this quote when I saw it written til I saw it come out her mouth [just] now 'cause DEAD A– SAME," she posted on Instagram.

LANA DEL REY

Speaking with *Pop Crave*, Chappell shared that Lorde, Ellie Goulding, and Lana Del Rey were the soundtrack of her adolescence. It's fitting, then, that she referenced the latter in her own lyrics: "When I sing that Lana song, it makes you cry," she sings in "Naked In Manhattan." (Chappell later admitted that the songs she was referencing were Lana's "Ride" and "Mariners Apartment Complex" both of which she has covered.)

LADY GAGA

It's no secret: Chappell loves Lady Gaga. "It was Gaga, and witnessing her at the age that I was, that was a domino effect of where I am now," she told BBC Radio. "Talk about fearless. Talk about charting new territory. It's so inspirational." She has previously explained to *Capital Buzz* that the spoken word intro to "Super Graphic Ultra Modern Girl" was inspired by Mother Monster's "Alejandro."

NICKI MINAJ

When *Dazed* asked what her favorite lyric of all time was, Chappell landed on a line from Nicki Minaj's "Itty Bitty Piggy." "I don't fuck wit pigs like As-salamu alaykum/ I put 'em in a field, I let Oscar Myer bake 'em," she recited.

"Chappell is the ultimate paradox— a revivalist of 1970s and '80s rebellion culture but also a trailblazer whose music is of the moment (and the future). As a teenager in a time of increasing restriction, I'm drawn to her. She's a symbol of free expression and self-confidence. I admire the way she continues to deface the pop industry's antiseptic reputation by incorporating glamour and drag, making pop music that's more nuanced than simple songs about heartbreak. It's also inspiring to see a queer icon dominate pop music. She publicly defends marginalized groups and brings important political discussions to pop. That's revolutionary! As a young musician myself (I'm 13), I'm grateful for what she's done for the future of art and artists."

—Penelope Whitbourne, student

For her MTV VMAs debut on September 11, 2024, Chappell wore a leather-and-brass, armor-inspired bodysuit by designer Zana Bayne. She's thought to be channeling Joan of Arc (the young French martyr who led a crusade for liberation and was burned at the stake) or Julie D'Aubigny (a sword-wielding opera singer in 17th century France). Introduced by drag icon Sasha Colby, Chappell lit up the stage with her performance of "Good Luck, Babe!"

Chappell's 2024 MTV VMAs performance of "Good Luck, Babe!" burned with talent, creativity, and yep, pyrotechnics.

"People are just now taking me seriously. [I'm] like, you know what, bitch? I've been doing this shit."

—Chappell to *Rolling Stone,* 2024

Chappell's performance persona is over-the-top in the best ways. She's been open about tapping into the "drag queen" that lives within her. "[The persona is] very larger-than-life. Kind of tacky, not afraid to say really lewd things," she told *Vanity Fair* in 2023. As *Wonderland Magazine*'s Sofia Ferreira observed after Chappell's sold-out show on September 21, 2024, at London's O2 Academy Brixton (right), there's a nostalgic and raw allure to Chappell's stage presence. "It feels as if we're watching a high-school band rehearsing in their parents' garage," she wrote. "Roan ran, jumped, serenaded a wig in best Steven Tyler–style… we're spectators of a singer who, along with her bandmates, is having the time of her life on stage."

Chappell closed out Week 1 of Austin City Limits at Zilker Park on October 6, 2024, with pyro, fittingly Texan flair, and plenty of "Pink Pony" energy. The performance was purported to be the largest in the music festival's history. During her set, seasoned with a punk edge and rock and roll–inspired fashion, she sang a spirited rendition of Heart's "Barracuda," which had fans clamoring for a studio version.

Surrounded by lively dancing rodeo clowns while riding atop a cartoonish—yet appropriate—pink pony, Chappell delivered a performance worthy of pop's new princess at the 2025 Grammy Awards. The rendition of "Pink Pony Club" was a fitting and heartfelt tribute to Los Angeles, where Chappell found her professional and personal footing and where she now lives. She has said that a night at the iconic West Hollywood gay bar The Abbey inspired "Pink Pony Club," and the whimsical experience influenced the energy she brought to her Grammys debut. "It's something that I couldn't really have experienced here in Missouri—in my small town at least," Chappell told *Headliner* about The Abbey in 2020. "It was completely eye opening and changed my direction from that point on."

At the 2025 Grammys, Andrea Ferrero played the famous "Pink Pony Club" guitar solo on a custom Gibson Les Paul six-string.

At Hinterland Music Festival in St. Charles, Iowa, on August 4, 2024, Chappell gave a wink and a nod to the Sisters of Perpetual Indulgence.

Her Superpower

GLEEFUL REBELLION

CHAPPELL TAUGHT US HOW TO *Dissent*

SAMANTHA OLSON
assistant news editor, *Cosmopolitan*

STOP being "creepy," Chappell Roan took to social media to tell her fans in August 2024, after one grabbed her and kissed her in a bar. In another incident, police at LAX intervened when a fan insisted on an autograph at the airport. In October 2024, Chappell stopped posing for photos at the premiere of the *Olivia Rodrigo: Guts World Tour* concert special to confront a photographer who had yelled at her at a Grammys after-party a few months earlier. She wanted an apology before loudly warning him, "Don't do that to an artist again."

This wasn't the first time Chappell had interrupted a step-and-repeat (a press opportunity at events) to tell off a photographer. Of course, the Internet had its opinions. Though some argued her reaction was "too much," others praised Chappell for standing her ground. "Actually love seeing women confront men who have wronged them in a society where women are taught to just take mistreatment quietly and with a smile," one fan wrote. "She makes me want to stop being a coward. Thank you, Chappell Roan."

So let's be real: Treating famous young women like this is the norm, but it's all too rare to see a celeb stand up for herself so publicly. I was 8 years old when the *New York Post* declared a night out for Britney Spears, Lindsay Lohan, and Paris Hilton a "bimbo summit." That's how I learned what the word *bimbo* meant. I saw Britney shamed for experiencing mental illness, Paris mocked for having sex, and Amy Winehouse ridiculed for struggles with addiction. During my childhood, it was normal for public figures to be harassed by the media—and it was normal for only men to be cheered when they clapped back. Creeps, stalkers, and cruel photogs were a fact of life for public-facing women who were told to be grateful we were paying attention to them at all.

But something shifted for me in September 2024, when I heard a photographer tell Chappell to "shut the fuck up" on the MTV VMAs red carpet. She yelled back at him, saying, "You shut the fuck up. Don't. Not me, bitch." As soon as it went down, I was transfixed. Here was a famous young woman standing up for herself in real time. At that moment, I thought about how my mom would yell at middle school bullies who harassed my sisters and me. I can't remember what they were bullying us for, but I do remember that we were so embarrassed by my mom's very public clapback. Often, the path of least resistance—saying nothing and moving along—seems like the best option to protect our peace. But watching Chappell stand up for herself, I saw another woman willing to stand up for herself, refusing to accept disrespect.

Although debate swirls about how famous women should deal with abuse or harassment from paparazzi, there is no

The top female stars of the early aughts—like Lindsay Lohan, Britney Spears and Paris Hilton (here in 2006)—were expected not to complain, however poorly the press treated them.

question that it's rampant. In my role as a news editor at *Cosmopolitan* covering pop culture, I've heard grown men make sleazy, overtly sexual comments about famous musicians and actresses dozens of times. Still, I couldn't bring myself to confront them. I was afraid of how they'd respond. I was scared that other journalists or photographers in the room would think I was difficult or ungrateful for my job. Looking back, I wish I'd acted more like my mom or Chappell and called out their behavior.

When I was young, stars like Britney and Amy had no choice—they struggled in silence to protect their public images. It wasn't until 2023—16 years after she infamously shaved her head and chased paparazzi with an umbrella—that Britney was able to speak openly about her miserable experience in the public eye. "[I] had people telling me what they thought of my body since I was a teenager," she wrote in her memoir, *The Woman in Me*. "Shaving my head and acting out were my ways of pushing back." The lesson for young Britney admirers like my friends and me was as simple as it was destructive: Smile, nod, say "thank you" for any attention, even when it's abusive. We wrongfully accepted that behavior as normal. It couldn't be further from the truth.

I hate how long it's taken for public-facing women to push back against this toxic attention, but I'm thrilled it's finally happening. Last year, Phoebe Bridgers kindly asked people to leave her alone at the airport while she was traveling to her father's funeral. When they, again, followed her through LAX with a camera, she doubled down on her point in an interview with *Rolling Stone*: "There's a way to [be a fan] without filming me without my permission behind the back of my head, chasing me down the street."

When women in the public eye firmly push back, they remind me there isn't always strength in silence. Showing up for yourself won't set you back where it matters. Whether you're a rising star on a red carpet or an up-and-coming writer trying to gain experience, Chappell, Phoebe—and, of course, my mom and older sisters—have taught me that keeping the peace is never worth being disrespected. †

At the L.A. premiere of *Olivia Rodrigo: Guts World Tour* on October 25, 2024. Chappell (right) confronted a photog who yelled at her previously.

When her privacy was invaded while mourning, Phoebe Bridgers (below on March 8, 2023) was vocal about her boundaries.

"I think, actually, I'd be more successful if I was OK wearing a muzzle."

–Chappell to the BBC, 2025

Chappell is never one to shy away from standing up for what she believes in. In a much-discussed moment from the 2024 MTV VMAs red carpet, the pop star clapped back at a photographer after he reportedly told her to "shut the fuck up." While posing for pictures, she turned around and said to the unidentified photographer while pointing her finger directly at him: "You shut the fuck up. Don't. Not me, bitch." Those who witnessed the exchange cheer Chappell on. In a separate interview with *Entertainment Tonight* later in the evening, she stood by her words. "This is quite overwhelming and quite scary," she explained. "For someone who gets a lot of anxiety around people yelling at you, the carpet is horrifying, and I yelled back. You don't get to yell at me like that." Celebs rallied behind her on social media after a video of the incident went viral.

"I'm not complaining about success. I'm just complaining about creepy behavior."

–Chappell on *Call Her Daddy,* 2025

On September 13, 2024, Chappell (quite literally) kicked off the second European leg of the Midwest Princess Tour at England's Manchester Academy.

MUSICIANS WHO STOOD UP FOR CHAPPELL

These stars have shown that they've got her back. BY SAMANTHA OLSON AND CHELSEY SANCHEZ

CHARLI XCX

Chappell told *Rolling Stone* that a number of pop stars—including Lady Gaga, Katy Perry, and Lorde—had offered advice on dealing with the pressures of fame, But it was Charli XCX (then in the middle of a huge moment thanks to her 2024 album, *Brat*) who was one of the first to check in on Chappell after a series of TikToks highlighted fans crossing personal boundaries.

MILEY CYRUS

In an interview with *Harper's Bazaar*, Miley defended Chappell from the intense public scrutiny that goes hand-in-hand with superstardom. "I wish people would not give [her] a hard time," Miley said. "It's probably really hard coming into this business with phones and Instagram. That wasn't always a part of my life, and I'm not a part of it now. I don't even have my Instagram password."

ROBERT SMITH

The Cure's lead singer reflected on celebrity's dark side on the BBC podcast *Sidetracked*. When asked about Chappell's boundary-setting, Smith explained, "I think what you're doing as an artist, you want people to feel like they're engaging with you. But it is a modern-world phenomenon that there's a sense of entitlement that didn't used to be there amongst fans." He continued, "It's horrible being gawked at all the time and prodded and poked and people expecting more of you."

HAYLEY WILLIAMS
After Chappell posted a message to Instagram asking fans for respect after experiencing "nonconsensual physical and social interactions," the Paramore frontwoman took to her own social media to show her support. "This happens to every woman I know from this business, myself included. Social media has made this worse," wrote Williams. "I'm really thankful Chappell is willing to address it in a real way, in real time. It's brave and unfortunately necessary." Chappell told *Rolling Stone*, "Hayley Williams is the strongest bitch ever."

NOAH KAHAN
After Chappell's MTV VMAs red-carpet moment went viral, singer Noah Kahan reflected on his own experiences with belligerent photogs. "I'll never forget leaving [the] Clive Davis [pre-Grammys gala] and the horrific shit photographers and paparazzi or whatever were saying to me in front of my sweet mom who couldn't believe it," he wrote on X. "Love this @ChappellRoan way to stand up for yourself." Kahan clarified that while most photographers are respectful, "There are some parasites who intentionally instigate."

HALSEY
After *The Hollywood Reporter* published an op-ed that criticized Chappell's Grammy acceptance speech, Halsey came to her defense: "I hope you're embarrassed of the absolute personal attack that you've ran and disguised as critical journalism. ...Our industry is comprised of thousands of voices, the elite at the very top of the class are not the example of a monolithic experience for all artists."

Brandi Carlile and Chappell (left) followed their own dress code at *Spotlight: A Night With Chappell Roan and Daniel Nigro*, moderated by Carlile at the Grammy Museum in Los Angeles on November 7, 2024.

Getting by with a little help from her friends! Tyla and Chappell got cheeky at the 2024 MTV Video Music Awards at UBS Arena on September 11, 2024, in Elmont, New York (top right). The same night (bottom right), she hung out with Shaboozey, Teddy Swims, and Quavo.

At the Grammy Awards on February 2, 2025, at Los Angeles' Crypto.com Arena, Chappell (top) embraced Billie Eilish, who received seven noms, and Sabrina Carpenter, who won Best Pop Vocal Album for *Short n' Sweet* and Best Pop Solo Performance for "Espresso." She also stopped to chat with Beyoncé—who was awarded Album of the Year for *Cowboy Carter*—and her daughter Blue Ivy Carter.

Amid the Grammy festivities, Chappell posed with Janelle Monáe, who channeled Michael Jackson sartorially and in her performance of "Don't Stop 'Til You Get Enough" (right). At another point during the evening, Taylor Swift, who has literally grown up in the public eye, whispered (some wisdom?) in Chappell's ear.

NO REALLY, *Good Luck* BABE!

by Dibs Baer
entertainment reporter and author

I CAN'T remember where I was the first time I heard the "Pink Pony Club" lyric "I heard that there's a special place, where boys and girls can all be queens every single day," but I remember that I cried.

Representation matters. Especially in an era where the powers that be are trying to erase trans people. "Pink Pony Club" may be Chappell's epic anthem—it's so mainstream, brides are dancing down the aisle to it—but "Good Luck, Babe!" is the song that speaks to me the most. In a nutshell, a queer girl denies her romantic feelings for another woman and inevitably ends up with a man. And Chappell is basically like, alrighty then, you can kiss a hundred boys in bars, you can say it's just the way you are, but that will never compare to what we have. Good luck trying to stop the feelings we have for each other and that you probably have for girls in general.

I'm a Gen X gay. What that means is that as a 55-year-old trans/nonbinary person, the first half of my life was spent in the closet because that's what we all did back then. We didn't really have a choice. We also didn't have a choice when it came to music.

We didn't have a pu pu platter of queer artists to choose from like today's generation—Fletcher, Reneé Rapp, Kehlani, in addition to Chappell, who's taken singing unapologetically about her queer life to a mind-blowing level. In my formative years, zero music existed that openly encapsulated my queer existence. It was always about men loving women and vice versa. You could read between the lines and pray that Whitney Houston was really a lesbian, but you never knew for sure. Indigo Girls and Melissa Etheridge kicked down the mainstream door, but neither dared to use 'she' pronouns until much later in their careers. Let me tell you, being excluded in literally every song that has ever existed makes you feel a type of way that isn't good—weird, lonely, even suicidal. That's not hyperbole.

What I love the most about "Good Luck, Babe!" is that dating a straight girl or boy is a canon event for pretty much anybody in the LGBTQ+ community. Almost all of us have done it. And now we have our own song about it! And still, life continues to imitate art. You would think after five decades on this planet, I'd stop doing stupid things, but you'd be wrong.

I recently fell—not for the first time—for a straight girl. We were on a Panama Canal cruise. When this straight woman inevitably said to me, "I can't" and "It's just the way I am," I sent her "Good Luck, Babe!" on Apple Music because, like I said, I'm Gen X.

My sweet situationship was so straight, she had never even heard of Chappell. Cue groaning. After listening to it, she texted me, "It's us!"

Yes, my lovely, it's us. Well, it was us. We were doomed, and now we're done. Sigh.

I hope when she misses me, she puts on "Good Luck, Babe!" and thinks of me fondly, especially when she's lying next to some dude in the middle of the night, with her head in her hands, nothing more than his wife. I hate to say I told her so... but I love to say thank God for this song. Thanks, Chappell. †

Melissa Etheridge rose to prominence with a string of hits starting in the late 1980s. She came out publicly in 1993, at the Triangle Ball, an event for gays and lesbians celebrating President Bill Clinton's inauguration.

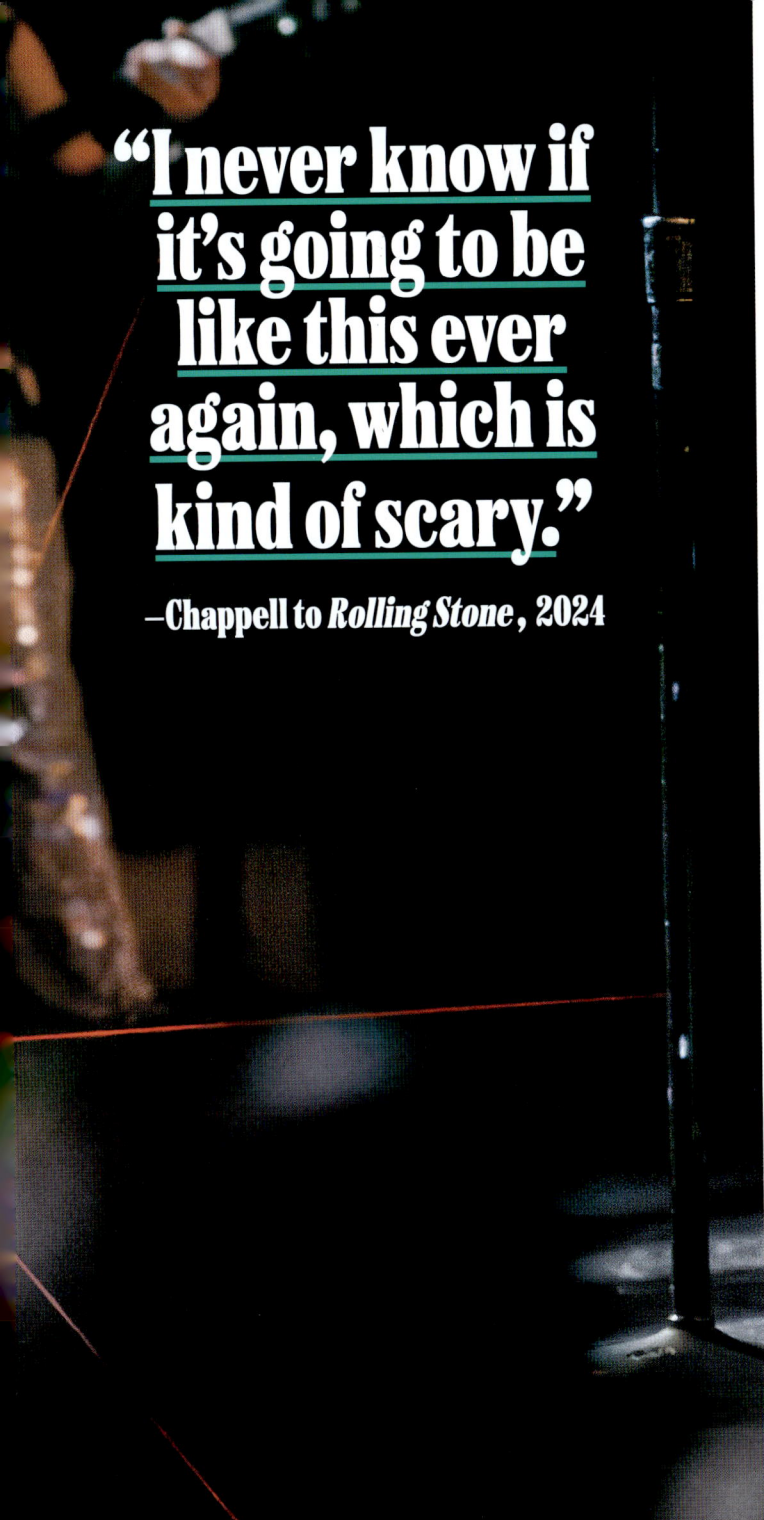

"I never know if it's going to be like this ever again, which is kind of scary."

—Chappell to *Rolling Stone*, 2024

Chappell—here with bassist Aubrey Harris at The Fonda Theatre in Los Angeles on March 15, 2023, during the Naked in North America Tour—has been frank about the demands of touring. In May 2023, she wrote on Instagram and TikTok: "I feel emo right now and just wanted to share that I am very fortunate and grateful to have my dream job. This job is very difficult for me to process and maintain a healthy life & mindset. I already have difficulty regulating my emotions because I have bipolar 2 disorder. ... Everything is very exciting right now and I'm realizing that success actually makes me quite uncomfortable and self-conscious and I'm not sure why yet. If ur an artist (indie or not) this career is fucking hard, and I feel you."

While accepting her Moonman for Best New Artist at the MTV VMAs on September 11, 2024, Chappell used her platform to give back to the communities that have fueled her success. In a heartfelt speech written in her diary, she dedicated the award "to all the drag artists who inspire [her]," as well as "to queer and trans people that fuel pop." She added, "Thank you to the people who are fans, who listen to me, who hear me when I share my joy and my fears." She also took a moment to speak directly to queer kids from her home region of the United States who might be watching and seeing themselves in her. She said to uproarious cheers: "For all the queer kids in the Midwest watching right now, I see you, I understand you, because I'm one of you. And don't ever let anyone tell you that you can't be exactly who you want to be, bitch."

Though awards are meant to put the recipient's work in the spotlight, Chappell used her moment to shine a light on the experiences of others. During her acceptance speech for Best New Artist at the Grammy Awards on February 2, 2025, she emphasized the importance of artist equity and challenged record labels to take responsibility for the musicians they work with. "I told myself if I ever won a Grammy and I got to stand up here before the most powerful people in music, I would demand that labels and the industry profiting millions of dollars off of artists would offer a livable wage and health care, especially to developing artists," she said to cheers. Chappell noted that after being dropped from Atlantic Records during the pandemic, she struggled to get back on her feet because she had no prior job experience and lacked health insurance. "If my label would have prioritized artists' health, I could have been provided care by a company I was giving everything to," she continued, adding that a "livable wage and health insurance protection" are essential for artist survival. *Vogue* called the moment "the speech of the night," and in an interview with *The New York Times*, Lady Gaga commended Chappell for "speaking the truth."

"Chappell's lyrics speak to feelings that I'd had all my life, although I only recently came out, at age 44. Coming out at midlife was hard. As a bisexual person, and especially as a late bloomer, I worry a lot about being "queer enough." Am I a fraud if I spent decades ignoring that part of myself? If the only real relationships I've had are with men? Then I saw an interview in which Chappell talked about her own queer imposter syndrome. Turns out, she had never even kissed a woman when she wrote songs like "Red Wine Supernova," yet she was able to capture queer longing in a way that felt utterly authentic. That interview helped me recognize that there's not one "right" way to be queer; that your identity isn't made valid based on sexual experience or how long you've been out. Chappell's words and music have helped me feel less alone, and inspired me to embrace who I am."

—Jennifer Rainey Marquez, writer and editor

She may be outspoken, but the subtle statements Chappell makes with her art are sometimes just as loud. During her performance of "Naked In Manhattan" at Austin City Limits festival on October 6, 2024, she stayed cool in the Texas sun with a handmade fan emblazoned with the words "Trans rights!" It was painted pink, blue and white, the colors of the transgender flag. Chappell has used her festival sets to advocate for queer and trans communities and prioritizes creating a safe, inclusive environment at all her shows.

Wearing a camo ball gown, Chappell performed at FirstBank Amphitheater in Franklin, Tennessee, on October 1, 2024. To combat ticket scalping, Chappell's team canceled many re-sold tickets that exceeded face value and resold them via a lottery.

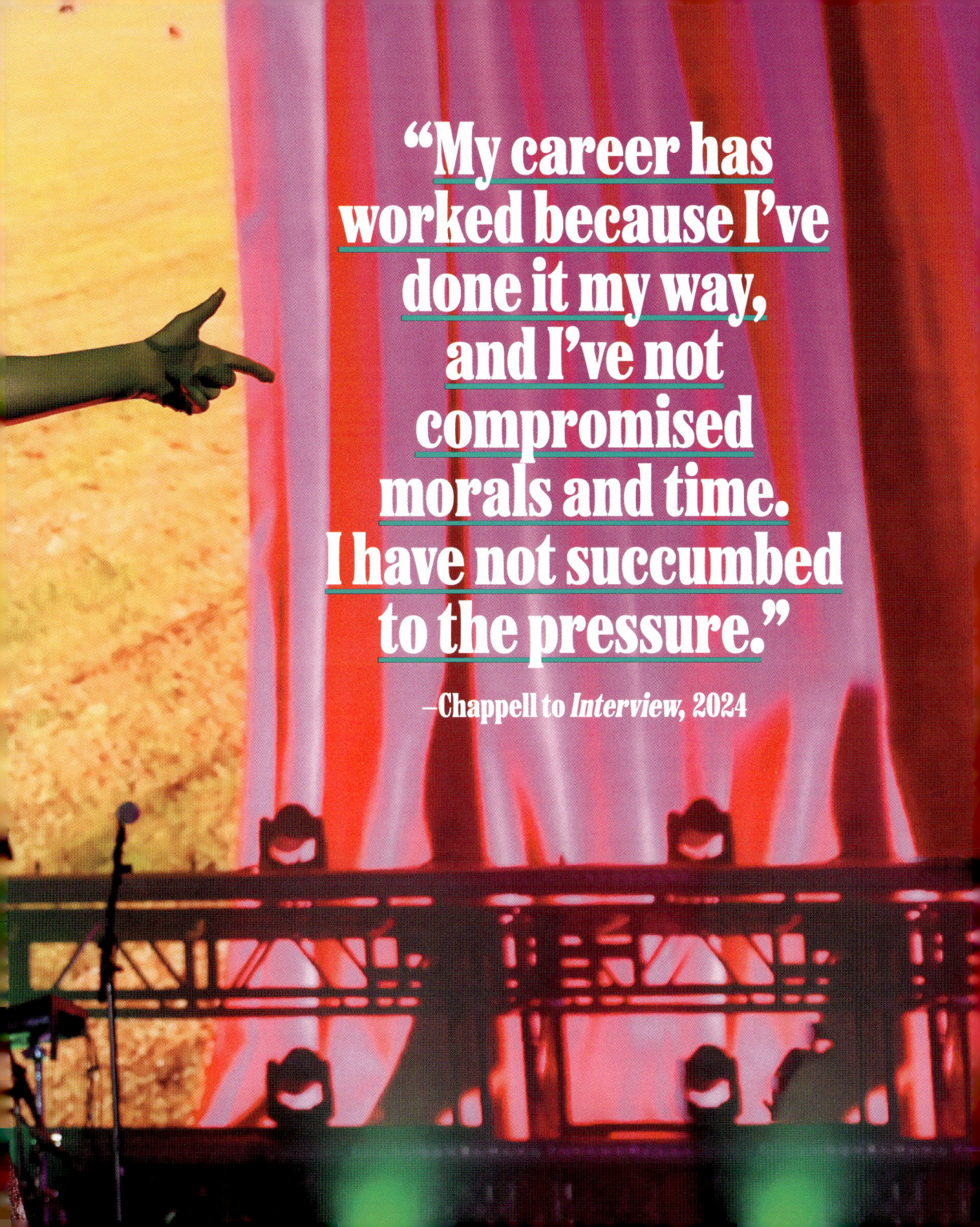

"My career has worked because I've done it my way, and I've not compromised morals and time. I have not succumbed to the pressure."

—Chappell to *Interview*, 2024

"Chappell's commitment to authenticity reeled me in. As I was completing my senior year of college, a time filled with change, confusion, and big decisions, Chappell accompanied me, reminding me to be true to myself. She uses her platform to speak out about issues that are important to her without fear of retribution. She's shown that unbridled joy can be accompanied by sincere activism work. And she demonstrates that the most fulfilling form of success comes from authentic self-expression and standing up about injustices you witness. I've been more determined to make my own voice heard ever since I discovered hers."

–Katherine Conlon, graduate student

Florida's conservative political climate was no match for Chappell, who fans flocked to see at Revolution Live in Fort Lauderdale on October 26, 2023. Local drag queens Suzie Toot and Kat Wilderness opened, and the crowd dressed scantily in keeping with the show's theme, "My Kink Is Karma."

Extra cheese, please! Chappell's devotees hold "Hot to go!" boxes at Governors Ball at Flushing Meadows Corona Park on June 9, 2024, in New York City. It's a favorite audience ritual, she explained to *Capital Buzz* in 2024. "Every show, someone brings a Papa John's box, and starts waving it around in the air."

A tiara-topped fan and her pup, dressed as the Midwest Princess, led the pack at the Haute Dog Howl'oween Parade on October 27, 2024, in Long Beach, California.

Pink-clad fans from coast to coast turned out during the summer of Chappell: at Governors Ball at NYC's Flushing Meadows Corona Park on June 9, 2024 (top); and at Outside Lands Music Festival on August 11, 2024, in San Francisco (bottom). Chappell's crowds are much larger than they used be, but unity among her audience has only grown. Maybe one reason is that "she's really thoughtful about the experience for fans," as her manager, Nick Bobetsky, told *The New York Times* in 2024. "Venue selection, parts of town, gender-neutral bathrooms… really creating a safe space."

"I feel like I moulted out of an old skin and I'm a new woman! I'm not that teenage girl anymore, but she's the reason why I am where I am now."

–Chappell to the BBC, 2024

Chappell fluffed her curls backstage before the show at Chicago's House of Blues on October 5, 2023, during her Midwest Princess Tour.

Copyright © 2025 by Hearst Magazine Media, Inc.
All rights reserved.

JACQUELINE DEVAL VP, Publisher
NICOLE FISHER Deputy Director
MARIA RAMROOP Deputy Managing Editor
LAURENE CHAVEZ Art Director
CINZIA REALE-CASTELLO Senior Photo Editor

Produced by Kalehoff Creative, LLC
LAURA KALEHOFF Editorial Director
PATRICK CROWLEY Creative Director
REBECCA KIMMONS BELL Photo Director
JO ANN LIGUORI Copy Editor
JY MURPHY Researcher

Library of Congress Cataloging-in-Publication
Data Available on request

10 9 8 7 6 5 4 3 2 1

Published by Hearst Home, an imprint of
Hearst Books/Hearst Magazine Media, Inc.
300 W 57th Street
New York, NY 10019

Hearst Home, the Hearst Home logo, and Hearst
Books are registered trademarks of Hearst
Communications, Inc.

For information about custom editions, special
sales, premium, and corporate purchases:
hearst.com/magazines/hearst-books

Printed in Canada
978-1-958395-55-4

"She's a Femininomenon!" essay copyright
© by Jennifer Armstrong.

Scan the QR code to join the editors at Cosmopolitan for editorial exclusives and invite-only events or go to Cosmopolitan.com /club-cosmo!

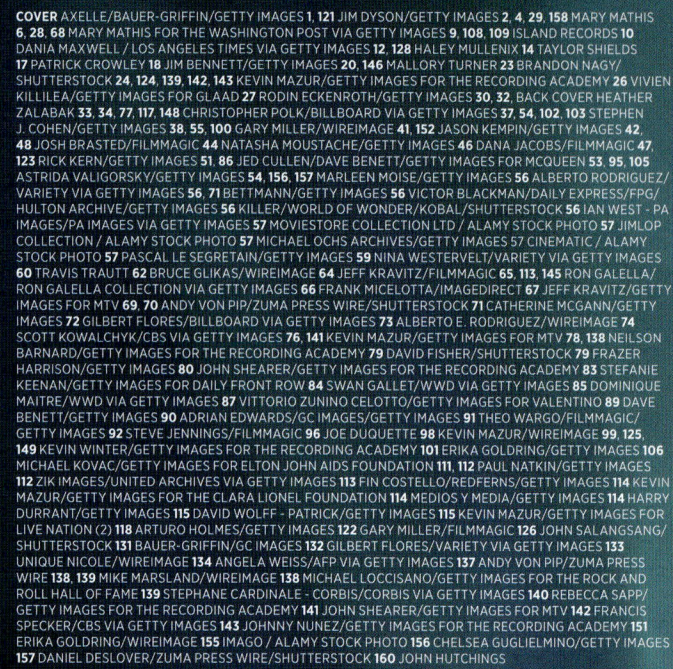

On the cusp of pop stardom, Chappell wowed a sold-out crowd at House of Blues in Boston on October 15, 2023.